P9-DMG-112

CLASSROOM
R·E·A·D·I·N·G
INVENTORY

CLASSROOM
R·E·A·D·I·N·G
INVENTORY

Sixth Edition

Nicholas J. Silvaroli
Arizona State University

WCB
Wm. C. Brown Publishers

Book Team

Editor *Chris Rogers*
Production Coordinator *Kay Driscoll*

WCB **Wm. C. Brown Publishers**

President *G. Franklin Lewis*
Vice President, Editor-in-Chief *George Wm. Bergquist*
Vice President, Director of Production *Beverly Kolz*
Vice President, National Sales Manager *Bob McLaughlin*
Director of Marketing *Thomas E. Doran*
Marketing Communications Manager *Edward Bartell*
Marketing Manager *Kathy Law Laube*
Production Editorial Manager *Colleen A. Yonda*
Production Editorial Manager *Julie A. Kennedy*
Publishing Services Manager *Karen J. Slaght*
Manager of Visuals and Design *Faye M. Schilling*

Illustrations by *Craig McFarland Brown.*

Permission to reproduce the Inventory Records is given freely to those who adopt this text for classroom use.

Cover design by Terri Webb Ellerbach

Library of Congress Catalog Card Number: 88–63679

ISBN 0–697–10421–4

Printed in the United States of America by Wm. C. Brown Publishers, 2460 Kerper Boulevard, Dubuque, IA 52001

10 9 8 7 6 5 4 3 2 1

Contents

Preface

The Classroom Reading Inventory (CRI), is designed for teachers and prospective teachers who have not had prior experience with informal reading inventories.

To become better acquainted with my version of an informal reading inventory, teachers and prospective teachers should:

1. Read the entire manual carefully.
2. Study the specific instructions thoroughly.
3. Administer the CRI to at least two students.
4. Keep in mind that successful individual diagnostic reading procedures are developed gradually through experience. Techniques, procedures, and ideas must be adapted to each testing situation.
5. Use the information gained from the CRI to plan an individual skills-oriented reading program.

I believe teachers and prospective teachers will begin to gain confidence with the CRI after administering this informal version seven times.

As a final note, let me express my gratitude to Ray Kimble, Bill Kirtland, Jann Skinner and Warren Wheelock, and recognize my indebtedness to them for their invaluable contributions to the development of the CRI.

Nicholas J. Silvaroli

Purpose of the Classroom Reading Inventory

Norm-referenced tests (group reading tests) are used to determine student reading achievement. This group testing approach might be called classification testing. The results classify students according to a global reading achievement level, which is frequently interpreted as a student's instructional reading level. The Classroom Reading Inventory (CRI), a version of an informal reading inventory, is an individual testing approach that attempts to identify a student's specific word recognition and comprehension skills.

Difference Between Individual and Group Testing

The difference between individual and group testing can be illustrated by a brief description of the reading performances of two fifth-grade students, Joan and Don. Their norm-referenced test (NRT) results are:

Joan (10 years 11 months old): NRT 4.3 overall reading
Don (11 years 2 months old): NRT 4.2 overall reading

When we examine their NRT results, these two fifth-grade students appear to be about the same in age and overall reading achievement. However, data obtained from their individual CRIs indicates that there are significant instructional differences between these two students.

On the Graded Word Lists of Part 1, Joan pronounced correctly all the words at all the grade levels, one through six inclusive. It is evident, therefore, that Joan is well able to sound out, or decode, words. However, when Joan read the Graded Paragraphs of Part 2, she was unable to answer questions about these paragraphs even at a primer-reader-level of difficulty.

Don, on the other hand, was well able to answer questions about these same paragraphs up to a second-grade reader level of difficulty. However, his phonetic and structural analysis or decoding skills were inadequate for his level of development.

The results obtained from NRTs concerning reading achievement tend to classify students as average, above average, or below average in terms of their reading achievement. As teachers however, we need much more specific information if we are to be able to develop meaningful *independent* and *instructional* reading programs for every student. The CRI is designed to provide teachers with just such specific and necessary information.

General Information

What Is the Classroom Reading Inventory (CRI)?

The CRI is a diagnostic tool for teachers to be used at either the elementary, junior high or middle school and high school or adult levels.

Form A and Form B—elementary (grades 1–6) level
Form C—junior high or middle school level
Form D—high school or adult level

All four forms are used to assess the student's ability to apply word recognition and comprehension skills, which are taught in the elementary grades. However, Forms C and D differ. Story content is believed more appropriate for junior high or high school students and adults.

Graded materials above the elementary reading level should not measure the reading skills taught at the elementary school level but should be concerned with higher level reading skills such as complex interpretations, advanced vocabulary, logic, speed, and application. Thus, the CRI merely adjusts the content or interest level for Forms C and D. The Graded Paragraphs used for all four forms of the CRI, are based on readability formulas[1] used in the development of basal readers. Therefore, the Graded Paragraphs of the CRI should be equivalent to the reading materials used in schools.

How Much Time Is Required to Administer the CRI?

The time required for administering the CRI is twelve minutes or less. To gain this time advantage, it was necessary to modify procedures usually found in other informal reading inventories. Among the modifications are that (1) only untimed responses to the Graded Word Lists are required; (2) the number of questions in the comprehension check per graded paragraph is limited to five; and (3) only oral reading is used, Part 2.

What Are the Major Uses for Each Form?

FORM A (pp. 31–65) is for elementary students (grades 1–6). It is designed to assess the students application of:

1. Word recognition skills
2. Comprehension skills
3. Spelling ability
4. Listening capacity (see p. 8 for a discussion of listening capacity)

1. Readability measures used in this inventory include:
   Dale, Edgar and Chall, Jeanne. *A Formula For Predicting Readability.* Bureau of Educational Research, Ohio State University, Jan. 1948, p. 11 (gds. 4-6).
   Flesch, Rudolf. *Marks of Readable Style.* Teachers College Columbia University, 1943 (gds. 6-7).
   Fry, Edward B. *Reading Instruction for Classroom and Clinic.* New York: McGraw-Hill Book Company, 1972, pp. 230-34.
   Space, George D. *Good Reading for Poor Readers.* Carrard Press, 1960, p. 116 (gds. 1-3).

FORM B (pp. 67–101) is an optional form for elementary students. Form B is similar in design but not content to Form A. Thus, Form B and Form A can be interchanged. The Graded Paragraphs in Form B may be used in any of the following ways:

1. As an additional set of oral paragraphs for posttesting
2. As a set of silent paragraphs for students who might reject oral reading
3. As a set of silent paragraphs to enable the teacher to give an oral paragraph and a corresponding silent paragraph for a more complete assessment of the student's overall reading achievement
4. As a set of paragraphs for assessing the student's listening capacity level

FORM C (pp. 103–131) is a new form designed for junior high school students. The administration, marking, scoring, and readability procedures are similar to those procedures used for Form A and Form B. However, the content is appropriate for junior high students.
     The major differences in Form C are:

1. The story content for all eight levels deals with mature topics.
2. Preprimer (PP) and Primer (P) levels are not included in the Graded Word Lists or Graded Paragraphs.
3. The Graded Word Lists, Part 1, include words for both seventh- and eighth-grade levels.
4. The Spelling Survey is not included.

FORM D (pp. 133–161) is designed for high school students and adults. The administration, marking, scoring, and readability procedures are similar to those procedures used for Forms A, B, and C. Form D is similar to Form C in that: the story content for all eight levels deals with mature topics; Preprimer (PP) and Primer (P) levels are not included; Graded Word Lists, Part I, include seventh- and eighth-grade levels; and a Spelling Survey is not included.

Can These Four Forms Be Interchanged?

Yes. Forms A and B can be interchanged for elementary students, and Forms C and D can be interchanged for older students. It is not recommended that Forms A and B be interchanged with either C or D.

Is the Inventory Used with Groups or Individuals?

Part 1 (Graded Word Lists) and Part 2 (Graded Paragraphs) are designed for use with individual students. Part 3 (Spelling Survey) may be used with the total class. The sections in this book titled Specific Instructions (pp. 7–15) explain how the parts of this inventory are to be administered.

Is the Teacher Expected to Test Every Student?

No. The inventory should be administered only to those students who need further testing in reading. Either the results of a norm-referenced test or the teacher's knowledge of the class group should reveal those students who appear to need further testing.

Background Knowledge Assessment

A student's background knowledge plays a crucial part in the reading comprehension process. As Taylor, Harris, and Pearson have stated: "People comprehend reading material by relating the new information in the text to their background knowledge."[1] It follows then, that the teacher should conduct a quick assessment of the student's background knowledge before the student is asked to read any Graded Paragraphs of Part 2. Additional information regarding background knowledge assessment is provided on page 8.

1. Taylor, B., Harris, L. and Pearson, P. D. *Reading Difficulties,* Random House, NY, 1988, p. 226.

Significant and Insignificant Errors

In 1982 Pikulski and Shanahan[2] reviewed research on informal reading inventories. One of their conclusions stated that "errors should be analyzed both qualitatively and quantitatively."

In the first five editions of the CRI, it was assumed that all word recognition errors recorded on the Graded Paragraphs of Part 2 were weighted equally. As such the teacher was asked merely to quantify word recognition errors. A new procedure is being introduced that requires the teacher to deal with not only just counting errors (quantitative) but to think about what the student is actually doing as he makes the error (qualitative). See: Specific Instructions, pp. 8–10.

In general, a word recognition error should be judged as significant if the error impacts or interferes with the student's fluency or thought process. Insignificant word recognition errors are minor alterations which do not interfere with student fluency or thought; e.g., student says *a* for *the* before a noun.

Helpful Hints (Based on questions teachers have asked over the past 20 years)

1. When administering the CRI, a right-handed teacher seems to have better control of the testing situation by placing the student to the left, thus avoiding the problem of having the inventory record forms between them.
2. When administering Part 2 (Graded Paragraphs), the teacher should remove the student booklet before asking the questions on the comprehension check. Thus, the student is encouraged to utilize recall ability rather than merely locate answers in the material just read.
3. The word count given in parentheses at the top of each paragraph in the inventory record for teachers, i.e., Form B, Part 2—Level 3 (96 words), does not include the title of the paragraph.
4. Readers living in different parts of the United States react differently to the Graded Paragraphs. If you or your students react negatively to one or more of the paragraphs, feel free to interchange the paragraphs contained in Form A and Form B or Form C and Form D.[3]
5. It is important to establish rapport with the student being tested. Avoid using words such as test or test taking, instead use working with words or saying words for me.
6. Before the teacher can analyze the types of word recognition errors a student can make, she will need a basic understanding of the word recognition concepts listed on the Inventory Record Summary Sheet, e.g., blends, digraphs, short vowels.
7. When a student hesitates or cannot pronounce a word in Part 2 (Graded Paragraphs), the teacher should quickly pronounce that word to maintain the flow of the oral reading.
8. Testing on the Graded Paragraphs of Part 2 should be discontinued when the student reaches the Frustration Level in either word recognition *or* comprehension.
9. Forms A and B are designed for elementary school children. Teachers are encouraged to use Forms A and B for pre-post testing, oral and silent paragraphs, and for listening capacity. Forms C and D are designed for older students and adults. Teachers are encouraged to use Forms C and D for pre-post testing, oral and silent paragraphs, and listening capacity.
10. Pictures have been eliminated from Forms C and D because it is believed that the Background Knowledge Assessment, used at the beginning of each oral paragraph, is all that is necessary to establish background for the story to be read.

2. Pikulski, John J. and Timothy Shanahan. "Informal Reading Inventories: A Critical Analysis" in *Approaches to Informal Evaluation of Reading,* edited by John J. Pikulski and Timothy Shanahan. Newark, Delaware: International Reading Association, 1982.

3. Form C and Form D paragraphs should not be substituted for Form A or Form B paragraphs.

11. The scoring guide on Part 2 of the inventory record for teachers causes some interpretation problems. For example, the guide for Form A, Part 2—Level 6, "A Beaver's Home," is as follows (See p. 60).

SIG WR Errors		COMP Errors	
IND	2	IND	0–1
INST	5–6	INST	1½–2
FRUST	11	FRUST	2½+

Should IND or INST be circled if a student makes three or four significant word recognition errors? It is the author's opinion that (a) if the student's comprehension is at the independent level, select the independent level for word recognition; (b) if in doubt, select the lowest level. This practice is referred to as undercutting. If the teacher undercuts or underestimates the student's instructional level, the chances of success at the initial point of instruction increase.

Part 1 Graded Word Lists *Form A and Form B*

Purpose To identify specific word recognition errors and to estimate the approximate starting level at which the student begins reading the Graded Paragraphs in Part 2.

Procedure Present the Graded Word Lists, starting at the preprimer (PP) level, and say:
"Pronounce each word. If you are not sure or do not know the word, then say what you think it is."
Discontinue at the level at which the student mispronounces or indicates he or she does not know five of the twenty words in a particular grade level (75 percent). Each correct response is worth five points.

As the student pronounces the words at each level, the teacher should record all word responses on the inventory record for teachers.[4] Corrected errors are counted as acceptable responses in Part 1. These recorded word responses may be analyzed later to determine specific word recognition needs.

Sample _____

1	was	saw	(error)
2	day	+	
3	three	DK (don't know)	(error)
4	farming	+	

After the student reaches the cut-off point (75 percent), the oral reading level should be started at the highest level at which he or she successfully pronounced all twenty words (100 percent) in the list.

Part 2 Graded Paragraphs *Form A and Form B*

Purpose
1. To estimate the student's independent and instructional reading levels. If necessary, estimate the student's frustration and listening capacity levels (see p. 8 for levels).
2. To identify significant word recognition errors made during oral reading and to estimate the extent to which the student actually comprehends what he or she reads.

Levels Four levels may be identified through the use of the Classroom Reading Inventory. These levels are independent, instructional, frustration, and listening capacity.

---

4. The Inventory Record for Teachers is a separate record form printed on standard 8½-by-11 inch paper. Note: teachers have the publisher's permission to reproduce all, or any part, of the inventory record for teachers, Form A pp. 51–62, Form B pp. 85–98, Form C pp. 119–131, and Form D pp. 149–161.

Independent Level

The teacher's first aim is to find the level at which the student reads comfortably.[5] The teacher will use the independent level estimate in selecting supplementary reading material and the library and trade books students will read on their own. Since this is the type of reading students will be doing for personal recreation and information, it is important that the students be given reading material from which they can extract content without risk of unfamiliar words and concepts.

Instructional Level

As the selections become more difficult, the student will reach a level at which he or she can read with at least 95 percent accuracy in word recognition, and with 75 percent comprehension or better. At this level the student needs the teacher's help. This is the student's instructional level,[6] useful in determining the level of textbook that can be read with teacher guidance.

Note: Considerable time is saved by not attempting to estimate the student's frustration and listening capacity levels. However, these levels are included in the event the teacher feels the need to obtain such data.

Frustration Level

When the student reads a selection that is beyond recommended instructional level, the teacher may observe symptoms of frustration such as tension, excessive finger-pointing, slow halting word-by-word reading, and so on. Comprehension will be extremely poor and usually most of the concepts and questions are inaccurately discussed by the student. This represents a level that should be avoided when textbooks and supplementary reading materials are being selected.

Listening Capacity Level

The teacher is asked to read aloud more difficult selections to determine whether the student can understand and discuss what was heard at levels beyond the instructional level. It is assumed that the reading skills might be improved through further instruction, at least to the listening capacity level.

Procedure Present the Graded Paragraphs, starting at the highest level at which the student recognized all twenty words in the word list, Part 1. Ask the student to read the story out loud and tell the student that you will ask several questions when he or she has finished.

Background Knowledge Assessment

Before the student is asked to read the story, the teacher should quickly assess the student's background knowledge. Each story in the CRI begins with a leading discussion statement called Background Knowledge Assessment. For example, in Form A, Part 2, level 1 the story deals with spiders (p. 21). The teacher is asked to say, "this story is about spiders. What can you tell me about spiders?" If the student merely responds with "I don't know" the teacher is asked to probe to determine if the student has some background knowledge about spiders. Such probes might include reference to T.V. or movies.

If the student has some knowledge of spiders the teacher should check the box for adequate. If after probes or other leading questions and the student exhibits no understanding, the teacher should check the box for inadequate. The story entitled "Red Ants" in Form B should be substituted for the Form A story.

Discontinue the Graded Paragraphs as soon as the student experiences frustration with either word recognition or comprehension.

Significant and Insignificant Errors

As stated earlier, word recognition errors should be judged on a qualitative and a quantitative basis. As such, this edition of the CRI introduces the qualitative concept of significant and insignificant word recognition errors. Prior editions of the CRI required teachers to simply count the number of word recognition errors without giving much thought as to what caused errors. In this edition, the teacher is asked to think about word recognition errors the student makes while reading and to determine if these errors are significant or insignificant. Only significant word recognition errors are to be counted (quantitative).

5,6. The actual number of significant word recognition and comprehension errors permissible at each graded level can be found in the separate inventory record for teachers.

The CRI recognizes the following five common word recognition errors and indicates the symbols used to represent them.

Common Error	Representative Symbol
Needs teacher assistance	P
Omission	◯
Substitution	——
Insertion	∧
Repetition	⌒

To enable teachers to make qualitative judgments some definitions and examples of significant and insignificant word recognition errors are provided. It would be virtually impossible however, to account for all possibilities. Therefore, the teacher is asked to use the following as a guide to establish his own criteria for establishing a qualitative mind-set in which to determine if word recognition errors are significant or insignificant.

Significant

The student word recognition error should be judged significant if the error impacts or interferes with the students fluency or thought process.

Examples:

1. Needs teacher assistance   P

   A clear significant error, student does not know how to pronounce the word.

2. Omission   ◯

3. Substitution   ——

   The sentence reads: "This black and green one is called a plant spider."

   The student reads:

   "This black and green one is called a plant spider." The student made two significant errors because they resulted in lack of sentence agreement (syntax confusion). These types of errors also lend themselves to insignificant errors. See examples later.

4. Insertion   ∧

   Insertions are rarely considered as significant errors because they tend to enhance what the student is reading, e.g., The trees look ∧ⁿ small. However, if the insertion changes the meaning of what is being read it should be judged as significant, e.g., The trees don't look small.

5. Repetition   ⌒

   Repetitions are rarely significant because it is believed that the student is merely repeating an easy word(s) while decoding a difficult word. However, if the student makes excessive repetitions (the teacher has to decide on the number), such behavior suggests the need for more reading practice and should be judged as significant.

Insignificant

Insignificant word recognition errors are minor alterations which do not interfere with student fluency or thought.

Examples:

1. Needs teacher assistance   P

   rarely insignificant

2. Omission   ◯

3. Substitution   ——

   The sentence reads: The birds are singing.

   The student reads: The birds are singing.
                                     is

"The bird is singing" The first error (omitted s), caused the second error, substituting is for are. If the student did not substitute is for are, language dissonance would occur. These errors might be judged insignificant if the idea of a single bird does not interfere with the overall meaning of the graded paragraph. Other examples of insignificant word substitutions are:

—The student interchanges a and the. This error is due to the fact that the student anticipates the article he knows he will find before a noun.
—The sentence, "How high we are," is read as "How high are we?" due mainly to the fact that the word "how" usually signals that the sentence will be a question.
—The sentence, "It is a work car." is read as, It's a work car." This is due mainly to the fact that it is more natural to say "it's" rather than "it is."

4. Insertion   ∧

   Sentence: "The trees look small." The student reads, "The trees look $\overset{so}{\wedge}$ small. This is an insignificant insertion because the student is reading in a spirited way.

5. Repetition   ⌢

   As stated earlier, repetitions should only be counted if they tend to be excessive. Again, the teacher must decide on what is excessive.

Marking Significant and Insignificant WR Errors (Part 2)

As the student reads each selection aloud, the teacher should use the previously mentioned symbols to mark both significant and insignificant errors:

Needs teacher assistance	P	Pronounce word for student
Omission	◯	Circle word(s)
Substitution	——	Add substituted word(s)
Insertion	∧	Add additional word(s)
Repetition	⌢	Mark over repeated word(s)

Sample

          is   *old*
It ~~was~~ the day to go to the ∧ farm.

                         P
"get in the bus," said Mrs. Brown

Marking Comprehension Responses (Part 2)

After each Graded Paragraph the student is asked to answer five questions. The separate Inventory Record for Teachers, label questions as follows:

(F) Factual or Literal

(I) Inference

(V) Vocabulary

Suggested Answers are listed after each question. However, these answers are to be read as guides or probable answers. The teacher must judge the adequacy of each response made by the student.

Partial credit (3/4, 1/2, 1/4) is allowed for all student answers to questions. In most cases it is helpful to record student responses if they differ from the listed suggested responses.

Scoring Guide

What follows is the actual scoring guide used for Level 5 (fifth grade), Form A p. 59.

Scoring Guide	Fifth		
SIG WR Errors		COMP Errors	
IND	2	IND	0–1
INST	5	INST	1½–2
FRUST	10	FRUST	2½

Note that the scoring guide for this fifth level (as well as all other levels in Part 2) uses error limits for the students. IND (independent), INST (instruction), and FRUST (frustration) reading levels.[7]

Thus, the guide suggests that when a student reads the Form A Level 5 selection entitled, "An Underwater School" and makes two SIG (significant) WR errors, the student is able to IND (independently) decode typical fifth-grade words. Five SIG errors instruction in WR is recommended. Ten SIG errors in WR at this level indicates that the student is frustrated.

The same procedure should be applied to the comprehension portion of the guide.

One final factor in the use of this guide. In order to arrive at a composite level both WR and COMP levels must be included. Therefore, in order for the student to be an independent reader at a given level, the student must be IND in *both* WR and COMP at the same level. The student needs instruction in either WR *or* COMP when one or the other occurs at a given level. The student should be judged as frustrated at a given level if he or she becomes frustrated in WR *or* COMP.

Summary of Specific Instructions

Step 1 Make the student comfortable. Complete the top of the Summary Sheet (name, grade, age, date, teachers and administered by) for the Form to be used. (See pp. 5–6 for helpful hints)

Step 2 Part 1, Graded Word Lists
(see p. 7 for purpose and procedure)

Step 3 Part 2, Graded Paragraphs

Step 4 Begin Part 2, Graded Paragraphs at the highest level in which the student knew all 20 words in Part 1.

7. See page 8 for a discussion of these levels.

Step 5   Background Knowledge Assessment (p. 8)

Before each Graded Paragraph engage the student in a brief discussion about the story to be read. Attempt to get the student to reveal what he or she knows about the topic and try to get the student to make predictions about the story. If the student has some background, rate student as adequate. If little or no background knowledge is apparent, mark inadequate and substitute the same level from another Form (A interchanges with B, C interchanges with D).

Step 6   Graded Paragraphs. Ask the student to read the selection aloud. Be sure the student understands that he or she will be asked to answer questions after each paragraph.

Step 7   Mark significant and insignificant WR responses. Ask questions and record student responses if they differ from suggested responses.

Step 8   When the student experiences FRUST (frustration) in either WR or COMP stop Part 2.

Spelling, Listening Capacity and determining
W.P.M. (words per minute) are optional and
generally not recommended for classroom use.

Step 9   Scoring WR responses. Make qualitative judgments regarding the student's significant and insignificant WR responses (see pp. 8–10) for suggestions.

Scoring COMP responses. Give full or partial credit for the student's responses to the question.

Scoring Guide. Count the number (quantitative) of WR and COMP errors and make the scoring guide per each level.

Step 10   Complete the Summary Sheet, and use information from Part 1 (percent per level) Graded Word Lists and data from each scoring guide to determine estimated levels (composite score). Combine WR and COMP results.

Part 3   Spelling Survey   *Form A and Form B*

Purpose   To obtain additional data on the student's ability to integrate and express letter-form, letter-sound relationships.

Procedure   Select a group of children who have completed Part 1 and Part 2. Begin at Level 1 (representative first-grade words). Level 2 is composed of representative second-grade words, etc.

Discontinue at the level at which five of the ten words are missed. It is recommended that the teacher administer only one or two levels at a given sitting. The results should be scored and analyzed after each administration. Students who have reached the cut-off point should return to their desks and study quietly.

Words Per Minute (W.P.M.)

Each level of Part 2 (Graded Paragraphs) includes a system for determining the student's words per minute (W.P.M.) while reading. This is optional and generally not recommended. However, it is included because some teachers find word-per-minute information useful.

To use this system, the teacher must find the number of seconds it takes the student to read at a given level. The number of seconds are then divided into the number under the division symbol. For example, Level PP gives the following symbol:

$$\frac{\text{W.P.M.}}{}\big/\overline{1440}$$

If it took the student 12 seconds to read the 24 words in "The Work Car" paragraph, the student would have read aloud this paragraph at the rate of 120 W.P.M.

Example:

```
      120 W.P.M.
12 / 1440
      12
      24
      24
```

The formula ($\underline{}/1440$ $^{W.P.M.}$) for each Graded Paragraph was developed by multiplying the number of words per paragraph (not including title) by 60. If the paragraph has 24 words we multiply by 60 and arrive at 1440 (words × seconds). By dividing by the number of seconds it takes the student to read aloud, the teacher is able to get an oral W.P.M. rate for each Graded Paragraph the student reads.

Specific Instructions

For Administering Form C and Form D
(To Be Used with Junior High School Students,
High School Students and Adults)

Part 1   Graded Word Lists   *Form C and Form D*

Purpose   To identify specific word recognition errors and to estimate the approximate starting level at which the mature student begins reading the Graded Paragraphs in Part 2.

Procedure   Present the Graded Word Lists, starting at Level 1, and say:

"Pronounce each word. If you are not sure, or do not know the word, then say what you think it is."

Discontinue at the level at which the student mispronounces or does not know five of the twenty words in a particular grade level (75 percent). Each correct response is worth five points.

As the student pronounces the words at each level, the teacher should record all word responses on the inventory record for teachers.[8] Corrected errors are counted as acceptable responses in Part 1. These recorded word responses may be analyzed later to determine specific word recognition needs.

Sample

1	her	his		(error)
2	fire	+		
3	frog	DK	(don't know)	(error)
4	garden	+		

After the student reaches the cut-off point (75 percent), the oral reading level should be started at the highest level at which the student successfully pronounced all twenty words (100 percent) in the list.

Part 2   Graded Paragraphs   *Form C and Form D*

Purpose
1. To estimate the student's independent and instructional reading levels. If necessary, estimate the student's frustration and listening capacity levels (see p. 8 for levels).
2. To identify significant word recognition errors made during oral reading and to estimate the extent to which the student actually comprehends what he or she reads.

---

8. The Inventory Record for Teachers is a separate record form printed on standard 8½-by-11-inch paper. Note: teachers have the publisher's permission to reproduce all, or any part, of the inventory record for teachers, Form C, pp. 119-131 and Form D, pp. 149-161.

Levels Four levels may be identified through the use of the Classroom Reading Inventory. However, most classroom teachers are concerned with independent and instructional levels. Teachers do this in order to reduce testing and scoring time. See page 8 for a description of the following reading levels.

Independent Level
Instructional Level
Frustration Level
Listening Capacity Level

Procedure Present the Graded Paragraphs, starting at the highest level at which the student recognized all twenty words in the word list, Part 1. Ask the student to read the story out loud. Tell the student that you will ask several questions when he or she has finished.

Background Knowledge Assessment Before the student is asked to read the story, the teacher should quickly assess the student's background knowledge. Each story in the CRI begins with a leading discussion statement called Background Knowledge Assessment. If the student has some knowledge of the selection to be read, check the box marked adequate and continue. If the student has little or no background knowledge, substitute a selection from Form D (if you're using Form C).

Discontinue the Graded Paragraphs as soon as the student experiences frustration with either word recognition or comprehension.

Note: See pages 8-10 for a discussion of significant and insignificant errors and a summary of specific instructions pages 11-12.

The Classroom Reading Inventory is designed to provide the teacher with a realistic estimate of the student's independent, instructional, frustration, and listening capacity levels in reading. However, merely identifying various reading levels is only slightly better than classifying the student on the basis of a norm-referenced test score.

The Classroom Reading Inventory is much more effective if the teacher is able to pinpoint consistent errors in word recognition and/or comprehension development. The Classroom Reading Inventory should enable the teacher to answer these specific questions:

Is the student having more difficulty with word recognition or comprehension skills?

Does the student have equal difficulty with both word recognition and comprehension skills?

If the student's difficulty is in the area of word recognition skills, are the problems with consonants, vowels, or syllables?

If the student's difficulty is comprehension, are the problems with fact, inference, or vocabulary questions? Is he or she a word caller?

Does the student appear to have other needs? Does the student appear to need glasses? Does the student appear to be anxious or withdrawn? Are high-interest/low vocabulary reading materials needed?

Following are two sample CRI records and a CRI practice work sheet. These examples are designed to help the teacher gain information on the scoring and interpretation of the Classroom Reading Inventory. Such information should enable the teacher to deal effectively with the type of questions presented above.

Example: Student with Inadequate Word Recognition Development

Mike B. is a fourth-grade student whose chronological age is nine years, two months. His full scale I.Q., as measured by the Wechsler Intelligence Scale for children, is 106, giving Mike a mental age of nine years, nine months. In his class, Mike is in the lowest reading group. His grade equivalency score in reading is 3.7, as measured by a standardized norm-referenced achievement test.

Mike's teacher, Ada Larson, administered Form A of the Classroom Reading Inventory to Mike. His summary sheet and graded word lists follow on pp. 17–18. Kindly note that Ada Larson decided not to continue with Part 2 of the CRI. Mike, a fourth-grade student, was experiencing problems with words at the beginning reading level. Therefore, this busy classroom teacher elected to save testing time and help Mike improve his word recognition skills.

Upon examination of Mike's summary sheet, we can see that he has problems with word recognition skills. He appears to have particular difficulty with endings and vowel sounds in the medial position (e.g., Mike read clumb for climb, trick for trucks, etc.).

Form A Inventory Record

Summary Sheet

Student's Name __Mike B.__ Grade __4__ Age (Chronological) __9-2__
Date __2/15/8__ School __Central__ Administered by __Ada Larsen__
yrs. mos.

Part 1 Word Lists			Part 2 Graded Paragraphs		
Grade Level	Percent of Words Correct	Word Recognition Errors	SIG WR	Comp	L.C.

Part 1 — Word Lists

Grade Level	Percent of Words Correct
PP	100
1 P	95
1	80
2	70
3	_____
4	_____
5	_____
6	_____

Word Recognition Errors

Consonants
____ Consonants
____ blends
____ digraphs
✓ endings
____ compounds
____ contractions

Vowels
____ long
✓ short
____ long / short oo
____ vowel + r
____ diphthong
✓ vowel comb.
✓ a + 1 or w

Syllable
____ visual patterns
____ prefix
____ suffix

Word Recognition reinforcement and Vocabulary development

Part 2 — Graded Paragraphs

Grade Level	SIG WR	Comp	L.C.
PP			
P			
1			
2			
3			
4			
5			
6			
7			
8			

Estimated Levels

	Grade
Independent	____
Instructional	____ (range)
Frustration	____
Listening Capacity	____

Comp Errors

_____ Factual (F)
_____ Inference (I)
_____ Vocabulary (V)
_____ "Word Caller" (A student who reads without associating meaning)
_____ Poor Memory

Summary of Specific Needs:

Mike needs word recognition training at the beginning reading level. Ability to recognize word endings appears to be a reasonable starting point.

*ND (not determined) Mike's teacher would have to give both Part 1 and Part 2 to establish estimated levels.

Form A Part 1/Graded Word Lists

PP		P		1		2	
1 for	+	1 was	+	1 many	+	1 sto<u>od</u>	*Stop*
2 blue	+	2 day	+	2 paint<u>ed</u>	*paint*	2 cl<u>i</u>mb	*clŭmb*
3 car	+	3 three	+	3 feet	+	3 isn't	+
4 to	+	4 farming	+	4 them	+	4 beautiful	+
5 and	+	5 bus	+	5 food	+	5 <u>waiting</u>	*want*
6 it	+	6 now	+	6 tell	+	6 head	*herd*
7 helps	+	7 read	+	7 her	+	7 cowboy	+
8 stop	+	8 children	+	8 please	+	8 high	+
9 funny	+	9 went	+	9 peanut	+	9 people	+
10 can	+	10 the<u>n</u>	*them*	10 cannot	+	10 mice	+
11 big	____	11 black	+	11 <u>eight</u>	*eat*	11 corn	+
12 said	____	12 barn	+	12 tr<u>ucks</u>	*trick*	12 everyone	+
13 green	____	13 trees	+	13 <u>garden</u>	*grade*	13 <u>strong</u>	*story*
14 look	____	14 brown	+	14 drop	+	14 I'm	+
15 play	____	15 good	+	15 stopping	+	15 room	+
16 see	____	16 into	+	16 frog	+	16 blows	+
17 there	____	17 she	+	17 street	+	17 gray	+
18 little	____	18 something	+	18 fireman	+	18 that's	+
19 is	____	19 what	+	19 birthday	+	19 thr<u>ow</u>	*thr—*
20 work	____	20 saw	+	20 let's	+	20 own	+
	_100_ %		_95_ %		_80_ %		_70_ %

18   CRI Interpretation

If you are unfamiliar with word recognition concepts in these word lists, you might refer to the following inexpensive programmed word learning materials for teachers.

Wilson, R. M. and Hall, Mary Anne. *Programmed Word Attack For Teachers*. Columbus, Ohio: Charles E. Merrill Co., 1984, 4th ed.

Example: Student with Poor Comprehension Development

Pamela T. is a fifth-grade student whose chronological age is ten years, six months. Her full scale I.Q., as measured by the Wechsler Intelligence Scale for children, is 98, giving Pamela a mental age of ten years, four months. In her class, Pamela is in the middle reading group. Her grade equivalency score in reading is 4.8, as measured by a group reading achievement test.

Pamela's teacher Wilbur Millston administered Form A of the Classroom Reading Inventory to Pamela. Her Summary Sheet follows on page 20.

Upon examination of Part 2 (Graded Paragraphs), it appears that Pamela's problem is with comprehension. She seems to have difficulty with inference and vocabulary questions. There is no problem with word recognition skills. Pamela might be called a word caller. She can sound out almost any word presented to her. However, she does not associate meaning with the words she decodes.

Again, if you are unfamiliar with how children develop comprehension skills in reading or what is meant by the term word caller, it is recommended that you refer to the textbook by Searfoss and Readence, 2nd edition, *Helping Children Learn to Read*.[9]

Note: Pamela began the Classroom Reading Inventory by responding to the Graded Word Lists in Part 1. Mr. Millston began Part 2 (Graded Paragraphs) at the last place Pamela had 100 percent, which was Level 2.

If Pamela had obtained IND in both WR and COMP, her teacher would go on to the Level 3 paragraph. Pamela was IND in WR, and INST in COMP; therefore, her teacher dropped back to the point where IND was reached for both WR and COMP (primer reading level). Level 3 is Pamela's upper-instructional level.

Teacher note: The Graded Paragraphs were started at Level 2. This was the last level at which Pamela T. successfully pronounced all twenty words (100 percent) on Part 1, Graded Word List. She evidenced comprehension difficulty: therefore, lower levels of Graded Paragraphs were used.

9. Searfoss and Readence, *Helping Children Learn To Read,* 2nd Edition, Prentice-Hall, 1989. Chapter 8, pp. 256–299.

Form A Inventory Record

Summary Sheet

Student's Name __Pamela T.__ Grade __5__ Age (Chronological) __10-6__ yrs. mos.

Date __2/15/85__ School __Central__ Administered by __W. Millstron__

Part 1 Word Lists			Part 2 Graded Paragraphs			
Grade Level	Percent of Words Correct	Word Recognition Errors		SIG WR	Comp	L.C.
PP	100	**Consonants** ___ Consonants	PP			
1 P	100	___ blends	P			
1	100	___ digraphs	1	IND	IND	
		___ endings	2 →	IND	INST	
		___ compounds	3	IND	FRUST	
		___ contractions	4			
		Vowels	5			
		___ long	6			
		___ short	7			
		___ long/short oo	8			
2	100	___ vowel + r				
		___ diphthong				
		___ vowel comb.				
		___ a + 1 or w				
		Syllable				
3	95	___ visual patterns				
4	95	___ prefix				
		___ suffix				
5	95	**Word Recognition reinforcement and Vocabulary development**				
6	75					

Estimated Levels

	Grade
Independent	1
Instructional	2 (range)
Frustration	3
Listening Capacity	Not Determined

Comp Errors

___ Factual (F)

✓ Inference (I)

✓ Vocabulary (V)

✓ "Word Caller" (A student who reads without associating meaning)

___ Poor Memory

Comprehension problems needs help associating her experiences with print-she also needs help with inference questions and vocabulary questions.

Background Knowledge Assessment. This story is about spiders. What can you tell me about spiders?

adequate ☒[10]   inadequate ☐

Plant Spiders

There are all kinds of spiders.

This black and green one is called a plant spider.

A plant spider has small feet.

All spiders have small feet.

Plant spiders live in nests.

They soon learn to hunt for food and build new nests.

Scoring Guide   First

SIG WR Errors[11]   COMP Errors

(IND)	0	(IND)	0–1
INST	2	INST	1½–2
FRUST	4+	FRUST	2½+

Comprehension Check

(F) 1. _+_ Is there more than one kind of spider?
(Yes—many more)

(F) 2. _½_ What two things do plant spiders quickly learn?
(Hunt for food and build new nests)

(F) 3. _+_ What color was the spider in this story?
(Black and green)

(F) 4. _+_ What did the story say about the spider's feet?
(Small, little)

(I) 5. _+_ What does this spider probably eat?
(Insects, bugs)

10. Pam had adequate background knowledge therefore Mr. Millston checked the box marked adequate.

11. Pam did not make any significant WR Errors.

Background Knowledge Assessment. At a rodeo cowboys show their skill with wild horses and bulls. Have you ever seen a rodeo (real, movie, T.V.)? adequate ☒ inadequate ☐

The Rodeo

The people at the rodeo stood up.

They were all waiting for the big ride.

Everyone came to see Bob Hill ride Midnight.

Bob Hill is a top rider.

Midnight is the best horse in the show.

He is big and fast. Midnight is a black horse.

Can Bob Hill ride this great horse?

Scoring Guide   Second

SIG WR Errors		COMP Errors	
(IND)	0	IND	0–1
INST	3	(INST)	1½–2
FRUST	5+	FRUST	2½+

Comprehension Check

(F) 1. _+_ What did the people do?
(<u>Stood up</u> , were waiting, etc.)

(I) 2. _d.k._ [12]The people seemed to be excited, why?
(They wanted to see this great horse and or rider.)

(F) 3. _+_ What was the name of the horse?
(<u>Midnight</u>)

(F) 4. _+_ What did he (Midnight) look like?
(<u>Big</u> , black, strong, etc.)

(F) 5. _d.k._ Why do you think that Bob Hill was a good rider?
(The story said he was a top rider. He had practice.)

12. didn't know

Background Knowledge Assessment. Can you tell me the names of birds you have seen? What things can you tell me about these birds?　　　　　　　　　adequate ☒　　　　inadequate ☐

Smart Birds

Everyone knows that birds like to eat seeds and grain. Birds also like to eat little stones called gravel. Birds have to eat the gravel because they don't have teeth to grind their food. The gravel stays in the bird's gizzard which is something like a stomach. When the bird eats seed, the gravel and the seed grind together. All of the seed is mashed up.

Tame birds must be given gravel. Wild birds find their own gravel on the road sides. Now you can see how smart birds are.

Comprehension Check

(F)　1. ½　Name two things birds like to eat.
(Seeds , grain, gravel stones, sand)

(F)　2. + Why do birds have to eat sand or gravel?
(Grind their food)

(V)　3. d.k. What does the word "grind" mean?
(Crush, make smaller, etc.)

(I)　4. d.k. What do you think would happen to birds that can't get any gravel in their food?
(Probably die, get sick)

(I)　5. + A bird's gizzard works somewhat like what part of your body?
(Stomach)

Scoring Guide　Third

SIG WR Errors		COMP Errors	
(IND)	2	IND	0–1
INST	5–6	INST	1½–2
FRUST	11	(FRUST)	2½+

Linda P. is a third-grade student whose chronological age is nine years, three months. The Summary Sheet below has been partially completed. Parts 1 and 2, Estimated Levels, Consistent Word Recognition Errors, Consistent Comprehension Errors, and Summary of Specific Needs have been left blank. Analyze the Classroom Reading Inventory for Form A, Parts 1 and 2, located on pages 24–28. Complete the Summary Sheet and compare your responses with the author's responses on page 29.

Form A Inventory Record _____

Summary Sheet (Sample Exercise[13])

Student's Name _____*Linda P.*_____ Grade __*3*__ Age (Chronological) __*9-3*__
                                                          yrs. mos.

Date _____ School _____ Administered by _____

Part 1 Word Lists			Part 2 Graded Paragraphs			
Grade Level	Percent of Words Correct	Word Recognition Errors		SIG WR	Comp	L.C.
		Consonants	PP			
PP	_____	____ Consonants	P			
1 P	_____	____ blends	1			
1	_____	____ digraphs	2			
		____ endings	3			
		____ compounds	4			
		____ contractions	5			
		Vowels	6			
		____ long	7			
		____ short	8			
2	_____	____ long/short oo				
		____ vowel + r				
		____ diphthong				

Estimated Levels

	Grade
Independent	_____
Instructional	_____ (range)
Frustration	_____
Listening Capacity	_____

Part 1 continued:

____ vowel comb.
____ a + 1 or w

Syllable

3 _____   ____ visual patterns
4 _____   ____ prefix
                ____ suffix
5 _____   Word Recognition
                reinforcement and
6 _____   Vocabulary
                development

Comp Errors

_____ Factual (F)

_____ Inference (I)

_____ Vocabulary (V)

_____ "Word Caller"
      (A student who
      reads without asso-
      ciating meaning)

_____ Poor Memory

Summary of Specific Needs:

13. Answer the questions on the bottom of p. 27 after completing Linda P.'s Summary Sheet.

Form A Part 1/Graded Word Lists

PP		P		1		2	
1 for	†	1 was	†	1 many	†	1 stood	†
2 blue	†	2 day	†	2 painted	plant	2 climb	†
3 car	†	3 three	†	3 feet	†	3 isn't	d.k.
4 to	†	4 farming	farm	4 them	†	4 beautiful	†
5 and	†	5 bus	†	5 food	†	5 waiting	†
6 it	†	6 now	†	6 tell	†	6 head	†
7 helps	†	7 read	†	7 her	†	7 cowboy	cow
8 stop	†	8 children	†	8 please	†	8 high	†
9 funny	†	9 went	†	9 peanut	pannut	9 people	†
10 can	†	10 then	†	10 cannot	†	10 mice	†
11 big	†	11 black	†	11 eight	†	11 corn	†
12 said		12 barn	†	12 trucks	†	12 everyone	d.k.
13 green		13 trees	†	13 garden	grade	13 strong	†
14 look		14 brown	†	14 drop	†	14 I'm	†
15 play		15 good	†	15 stopping	†	15 room	†
16 see		16 into	†	16 frog	†	16 blows	†
17 there		17 she	†	17 street	say	17 gray	gay
18 little		18 something	†	18 fireman	†	18 that's	that
19 is		19 what	†	19 birthday	†	19 throw	†
20 work		20 saw	†	20 let's	†	20 own	†
	100 %		95 %		80 %		75 %

Teacher note: Stop Form A, Part 1—Graded Word Lists—as soon as the student misses five words in any one column. Begin Form A, Part 2—Graded Paragraphs, at the highest level at which all twenty words were recognized.

W.P.M.

/1440

Background Knowledge Assessment. This story is about work cars at the airport. Have you ever seen these work cars?

adequate ☒   inadequate ☐

The Work Car

"Look over there," said Jane.

"See the funny little car.

Can you see it?"

"I see it," said Bob.

"It is a work car."

Scoring Guide Preprimer

SIG WR Errors		COMP Errors	
(IND)	0	(IND)	0–1
INST	1–2	INST	1½–2
FRUST	3+	FRUST	2½+

Comprehension Check

(F) 1. _+_ Who were the children in the story?
(Bob and Jane)

(F) 2. _+_ What did they see?
(Funny little car)

(I) 3. _+_ Who saw the car first?
(Jane)

(F) 4. _+_ What was the car called?
(Work car or help car)

(I) 5. _+_ These little work cars go between the planes and the terminal building; what do they do?
(Carry baggage or luggage)

W.P.M.

/1980

Background Knowledge Assessment. Have you ever flown on an airplane? Tell me about it. (If not, what might it be like.)

adequate ☒   inadequate ☐

Jack's First Airplane Ride

Jack and his father got on the airplane.

Away they flew.

"We are up high," said Jack.

"The trees look small."

"And so do the animals," said Father.

Jack said, "This is fun!"

Scoring Guide Primer

SIG WR Errors		COMP Errors	
(IND)	0	(IND)	0–1
INST	1–2	INST	1½–2
FRUST	3+	FRUST	2½+

Comprehension Check

(F) 1. _+_ Who was with Jack on the airplane?
(Father)

(F) 2. _+_ What words in the story told that Jack liked his ride?
(This is fun!)

(V) 3. _+_ What did the word "high" mean in the story?
(Way up in the air , above the buildings, trees, etc.)

(I) 4. _+_ What in the story told you that Jack and his father were up high?
(The trees and animals looked small . They were flying.)

(F) 5. *d.k.* How many airplane rides did Jack have before this one?
(None)

Background Knowledge Assessment. This story is about spiders. What can you tell me about spiders?

adequate ☒   inadequate ☐

Plant Spiders

There are all kinds of spiders.

This black and green one is called a plant spider.
^P over "green"

A plant spider has small feet.

All spiders have small feet.

Plant spiders live in nests.

They soon learn to hunt for food and build (new) nests.

Scoring Guide First

SIG WR Errors		COMP Errors	
IND	0	(IND)	0–1
(INST)	2	INST	1½–2
FRUST	4+	FRUST	2½+

Comprehension Check

(F) 1. ✓ Is there more than one kind of spider?
(<u>Yes</u>—many more)

(F) 2. ✓ What two things do plant spiders quickly learn?
(<u>Hunt for food</u> and build new nests)

(F) 3. ½ What color was the spider in this story?
(Black and <u>green</u>)

(F) 4. ✓ What did the story say about the spider's feet?
(Small, little) **small ones**

(I) 5. ✓ What does this spider probably eat?
(Insects, <u>bugs</u>)

Answer the Following Questions:[14]

1. Significant WR errors are determined from student responses on Part 1, Graded Word Lists or Part 2, Graded Paragraphs? _____ .
2. Why were the words from 11 to 20, Part 1, PP skipped? _____ .
3. Given Linda P.'s responses on Part 1, what is the beginning starting level on Part 2?
_____ .
4. Linda P.'s background knowledge for this selection appears to be adequate. What should the teacher do if Linda lacked background information about Plant Spiders Level 1.
5. Discuss the significant and insignificant WR errors in the Rodeo selection (p. 28) Part 2, Level 2.

6. The Plant Spider selection (above) has 43 words. Is the title Plant Spider included in the word count?
_____ .

14. See page 28 for answers to these six questions.

Background Knowledge Assessment. At a rodeo cowboys show their skill with wild horses and bulls. Have you ever seen a rodeo (real, movie, or T.V.)? adequate ☒ inadequate ☐

The Rodeo

The people at the rodeo stood up. [P]

They (were) all waiting for the big ride.

Everyone came to see ~~Bob Hill~~ ride Midnight. [him] [P]

~~Bob~~ Hill is a top rider. [Bobby]

Midnight is the best horse in the show.

He is big and fast. Midnight is a black horse.

Can ~~Bob~~ Hill ride this great horse? [Bobby]

Scoring Guide Second

SIG WR Errors		COMP Errors	
IND	0	IND	0–1
INST	3	(INST)	1½–2
(FRUST)	5+	FRUST	2½+

Comprehension Check

(F) 1. ½ What did the people do?
(Stood up were waiting went to see show)

(I) 2. + The people seemed to be excited, why?
(They wanted to see this <u>great horse</u> and or rider.)

(F) 3. ✓ What was the name of the horse?
(Midnight)

(F) 4. + What did he (Midnight) look like?
(<u>Big</u> , black, strong, etc.)

(F) 5. + Why do you think that Bob Hill was a good rider?
(<u>The story said he was a top rider</u> . He had practice.)

Answers for Six Questions on Page 27

1. Part 2, Graded Paragraphs
2. Words 11–20 are as difficult as 1–10, therefore skipping them saves time.
3. Last place she had 100 percent on Part 1, therefore PP Level.
4. Substitute Red Ants, Level 1, Form B.
5. Needing assistance (P) with the words stood and Midnight interfered with Linda's ability to answer questions. Omitting the word were, interfered with syntactical structure. Substituting Bobby for Bob and repeating is the best, was not significant because these errors did not interfere with Linda's fluency or thought process.
6. No, title not included in total words in parenthesis.

Form A Inventory Record _____

Summary Sheet

Student's Name ___*Linda P*___ Grade __*3*__ Age (Chronological) __*9-3*__
                                                                    yrs. mos.
Date _____ School _____ Administered by __*N. Silvaroli*__

Part 1 Word Lists			Part 2 Graded Paragraphs			
Grade Level	Percent of Words Correct	Word Recognition Errors		SIG WR	Comp	L.C.
		Consonants	PP	*IND.*	*IND.*	
PP	*100*	___ Consonants	P	*IND.*	*IND.*	
1　P	*95*	✓ blends	1	*INST.*	*IND.*	
1	*80*	___ digraphs	2	*FRUST.*	*INST.*	
		✓ endings	3			
		✓ compounds	4			
		✓ contractions	5			
		Vowels	6			
		___ long	7			
		___ short	8			
2	*75*	___ long/short oo				
		___ vowel + r	**Estimated Levels**			
		___ diphthong			Grade	
		___ vowel comb.	Independent		*P*	
		___ a + 1 or w	Instructional		___ (range)	
		Syllable	Frustration			
3	____	___ visual patterns	Listening Capacity		*Not Determined*	
4	____	___ prefix				
5	____	___ suffix				
6	____	Word Recognition reinforcement and Vocabulary development				

Comp Errors	Summary of Specific Needs:
____ Factual (F)	
____ Inference (I)	*See paragraph below for discussion of Linda's reading needs*
____ Vocabulary (V)	
____ "Word Caller" (A student who reads without associating meaning)	
____ Poor Memory	

Linda is having difficulty applying word recognition skills. She appears to understand consonants and digraphs but needs to learn to apply the remainder of the consonant, vowel, and syllable skills. Linda comprehends what she reads but might experience difficulty with inference questions. She has an independent (IND) level of primer (P). Therefore, she should be encouraged to independently read at this level.

Form A
Part 1 Graded Word Lists

PP

1 for

2 blue

3 car

4 to

5 and

6 it

7 helps

8 stop

9 funny

10 can

11 big

12 said

13 green

14 look

15 play

16 see

17 there

18 little

19 is

20 work

P

1 was

2 day

3 three

4 farming

5 bus

6 now

7 read

8 children

9 went

10 then

11 black

12 barn

13 trees

14 brown

15 good

16 into

17 she

18 something

19 what

20 saw

1

1 many

2 painted

3 feet

4 them

5 food

6 tell

7 her

8 please

9 peanut

10 cannot

11 eight

12 trucks

13 garden

14 drop

15 stopping

16 frog

17 street

18 fireman

19 birthday

20 let's

2

1 stood

2 climb

3 isn't

4 beautiful

5 waiting

6 head

7 cowboy

8 high

9 people

10 mice

11 corn

12 everyone

13 strong

14 I'm

15 room

16 blows

17 gray

18 that's

19 throw

20 own

3

1 hour

2 senseless

3 turkeys

4 anything

5 chief

6 foolish

7 enough

8 either

9 chased

10 robe

11 crowd

12 crawl

13 unhappy

14 clothes

15 hose

16 pencil

17 meat

18 discover

19 picture

20 nail

4

1 spoon

2 dozen

3 trail

4 machine

5 bound

6 exercise

7 disturbed

8 force

9 weather

10 rooster

11 mountains

12 island

13 hook

14 guides

15 moan

16 settlers

17 pitching

18 prepared

19 west

20 knowledge

5

1 whether

2 hymn

3 sharpness

4 amount

5 shrill

6 freedom

7 loudly

8 scientists

9 musical

10 considerable

11 examined

12 scarf

13 muffled

14 pacing

15 oars

16 delicious

17 octave

18 terrific

19 salmon

20 briskly

6

1 sentinel

2 nostrils

3 marsh

4 sensitive

5 calmly

6 tangle

7 wreath

8 teamwork

9 billows

10 knights

11 instinct

12 liberty

13 pounce

14 rumored

15 strutted

16 dragon

17 hearth

18 shifted

19 customers

20 blond

Form A

Part 2 Graded Paragraphs
Designed for Elementary School Children (grades 1-6)

The Work Car

"Look over there," said Jane.
"See the funny little car.
Can you see it?"
"I see it," said Bob.
"It is a work car."

Jack's First Airplane Ride

Jack and his father got on the airplane.
Away they flew.
"We are up high," said Jack.
"The trees look small."
"And so do the animals," said Father.
Jack said, "This is fun!"

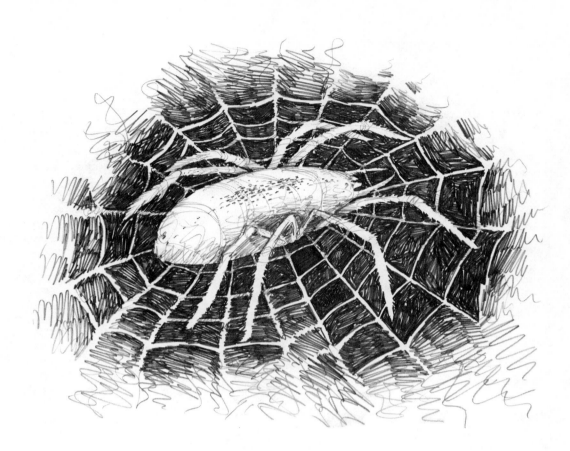

Plant Spiders

There are all kinds of spiders.
This black and green one is called a plant spider.
A plant spider has small feet.
All spiders have small feet.
Plant spiders live in nests.
They soon learn to hunt for food and build new nests.

The Rodeo

The people at the rodeo stood up.
They were all waiting for the big ride.
Everyone came to see Bob Hill ride Midnight.
Bob Hill is a top rider.
Midnight is the best horse in the show.
He is big and fast. Midnight is a black horse.
Can Bob Hill ride this great horse?

Smart Birds

Everyone knows that birds like to eat seeds and grain. Birds also like to eat little stones called gravel. Birds have to eat the gravel because they don't have teeth to grind their food. The gravel stays in the bird's gizzard which is something like a stomach. When the bird eats seed, the gravel and the seed grind together. All of the seed is mashed up.

Tame birds must be given gravel. Wild birds find their own gravel on the road sides. Now you can see how smart birds are.

Sky Diving

An exciting new sport in the world today is sky diving. Sky divers do tricks, make falls, and take interesting pictures. This sport takes you away from your everyday life into a wonderful world you have never known. It is almost like being in a dream. Once out of the airplane, you feel as if you can climb walls or float over mountains.

Sky divers work to develop each of their jumps. Men and women are interested in sky diving. In fact, more people learn to sky dive each year. This relaxing sport is one of man's newest adventures.

An Underwater School

Scientists wanted to prove that seals had excellent hearing. Blind seals were used in the study. The blind seals were trained to expect food when they heard sounds. The seals quickly learned to hear soft sounds at long distances. Fishermen who splash oars or make noises in water should think about this study.

The same experts also trained seals to tell the difference between two bell-tones. One bell-tone meant food; two bell-tones meant no food. When the seals made mistakes they were given a light tap. The seals were good learners. They easily learned to tell the difference between the bell-tones.

A Beaver's Home

A beaver's home, called a lodge, always has a flooded lower room. These homes are built in large ponds or streams. Mud and sticks are the main building materials. One room is built above the water level and another room is located under water. The only way a beaver can get into the house is to submerge and enter through an opening in the flooded room. This room serves two purposes: a storage area and a sanctuary from enemies.

Occasionally the lower room becomes dry because the beaver's dam has been destroyed. This energetic animal has to repair the dam quickly or begin building a new home in another place.

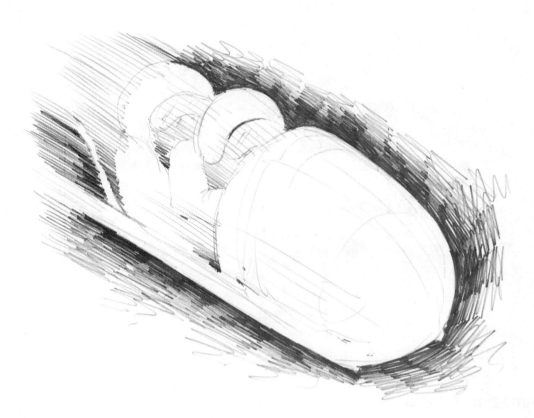

The Wildest Run in the World

The Van Hoevenberg bobrun near Lake Placid, New York, is the wildest run in the world. This bobrun is steep, icy, and extremely dangerous. It is almost a mile long and has sixteen sharp curves. High banked walls keep the bobsleds from hurtling off the bobrun.

Bobsleds used in competitive races are carefully designed. The lead person must be a skillful driver and the back person serves as the brakeman.

Most championship races at Lake Placid use four-person sleds. The riders bob back and forth together to make the sled go faster. That's how bobsleds got their name. Championship teams at Lake Placid have reached speeds in excess of ninety miles per hour.

Bobsledding has been an Olympic sport since 1924.

Amazing Amelia

Amelia Earhart worked to open up new careers for women. She might easily qualify as an early feminist. When World War I ended, there were still a great many fields closed to women. Despite this, Amelia decided to go to medical school. In 1919 it was very difficult for women to get into medical college. Amelia persisted and did get into medical school. After her first year of school Amelia decided to become a pilot.

After only ten hours of training, this amazing woman set a new world flying record. She flew to a height of over two miles.

Soon after this Amelia and an all male crew made a flight across the Atlantic Ocean. This record-breaking flight took exactly twenty hours and forty minutes.

Until her death in 1937, Amelia continued to challenge many things that were thought to be impossible.

Form A
Inventory Record for Teachers

Form A Inventory Record _____

Summary Sheet

Student's Name _____ Grade _____ Age (Chronological) _____

Date _____ School _____ Administered by _____ yrs. mos.

Part 1 Word Lists			Part 2 Graded Paragraphs		
Grade Level	Percent of Words Correct	Word Recognition Errors		SIG WR	Comp	L.C.

Grade Level	Percent of Words Correct	Word Recognition Errors				
PP 1 P 1	_____ _____ _____	Consonants ____ Consonants ____ blends ____ digraphs ____ endings ____ compounds ____ contractions	PP P 1 2 3			
2	_____	Vowels ____ long ____ short ____ long/short oo ____ vowel + r ____ diphthong ____ vowel comb. ____ a + 1 or w	4 5 6 7 8			
3 4	_____ _____	Syllable ____ visual patterns ____ prefix ____ suffix				
5 6	_____ _____	Word Recognition reinforcement and Vocabulary development				

Estimated Levels

	Grade
Independent	_____
Instructional	_____ (range)
Frustration	_____
Listening Capacity	_____

Comp Errors
_____ Factual (F)
_____ Inference (I)
_____ Vocabulary (V)
_____ "Word Caller"
     (A student who
     reads without asso-
     ciating meaning)
_____ Poor Memory

Summary of Specific Needs:

PP		P		1		2	
1 for	_____	1 was	_____	1 many	_____	1 stood	_____
2 blue	_____	2 day	_____	2 painted	_____	2 climb	_____
3 car	_____	3 three	_____	3 feet	_____	3 isn't	_____
4 to	_____	4 farming	_____	4 them	_____	4 beautiful	_____
5 and	_____	5 bus	_____	5 food	_____	5 waiting	_____
6 it	_____	6 now	_____	6 tell	_____	6 head	_____
7 helps	_____	7 read	_____	7 her	_____	7 cowboy	_____
8 stop	_____	8 children	_____	8 please	_____	8 high	_____
9 funny	_____	9 went	_____	9 peanut	_____	9 people	_____
10 can	_____	10 then	_____	10 cannot	_____	10 mice	_____
11 big	_____	11 black	_____	11 eight	_____	11 corn	_____
12 said	_____	12 barn	_____	12 trucks	_____	12 everyone	_____
13 green	_____	13 trees	_____	13 garden	_____	13 strong	_____
14 look	_____	14 brown	_____	14 drop	_____	14 I'm	_____
15 play	_____	15 good	_____	15 stopping	_____	15 room	_____
16 see	_____	16 into	_____	16 frog	_____	16 blows	_____
17 there	_____	17 she	_____	17 street	_____	17 gray	_____
18 little	_____	18 something	_____	18 fireman	_____	18 that's	_____
19 is	_____	19 what	_____	19 birthday	_____	19 throw	_____
20 work	_____	20 saw	_____	20 let's	_____	20 own	_____
	_____ %		_____ %		_____ %		_____ %

Teacher note: If the child missed five words in any column—stop Part 1. Begin Graded Paragraphs, Part 2, (Form A), at highest level in which child recognized all 20 words. To save time, if the first ten words were correct, go on to the next list. If one of the first ten words were missed, continue the entire list.

Form A Part 1

3		4		5		6	
1 hour	_____	1 spoon	_____	1 whether	_____	1 sentinel	_____
2 senseless	_____	2 dozen	_____	2 hymn	_____	2 nostrils	_____
3 turkeys	_____	3 trail	_____	3 sharpness	_____	3 marsh	_____
4 anything	_____	4 machine	_____	4 amount	_____	4 sensitive	_____
5 chief	_____	5 bound	_____	5 shrill	_____	5 calmly	_____
6 foolish	_____	6 exercise	_____	6 freedom	_____	6 tangle	_____
7 enough	_____	7 disturbed	_____	7 loudly	_____	7 wreath	_____
8 either	_____	8 force	_____	8 scientists	_____	8 teamwork	_____
9 chased	_____	9 weather	_____	9 musical	_____	9 billows	_____
10 robe	_____	10 rooster	_____	10 considerable	_____	10 knights	_____
11 crowd	_____	11 mountains	_____	11 examined	_____	11 instinct	_____
12 crawl	_____	12 island	_____	12 scarf	_____	12 liberty	_____
13 unhappy	_____	13 hook	_____	13 muffled	_____	13 pounce	_____
14 clothes	_____	14 guides	_____	14 pacing	_____	14 rumored	_____
15 hose	_____	15 moan	_____	15 oars	_____	15 strutted	_____
16 pencil	_____	16 settlers	_____	16 delicious	_____	16 dragon	_____
17 meat	_____	17 pitching	_____	17 octave	_____	17 hearth	_____
18 discover	_____	18 prepared	_____	18 terrific	_____	18 shifted	_____
19 picture	_____	19 west	_____	19 salmon	_____	19 customers	_____
20 nail	_____	20 knowledge	_____	20 briskly	_____	20 blond	_____
	_____ %		_____ %		_____ %		_____ %

‾‾‾‾ / 1440

Background Knowledge Assessment.   This story is about work cars at the airport. Have you ever seen these work cars?[16]   adequate ☐   inadequate ☐

The Work Car

"Look over there," said Jane.

"See the funny little car.

Can you see it?"

"I see it," said Bob.

"It is a work car."

Scoring Guide   Preprimer

SIG WR Errors		COMP Errors	
IND	0	IND	0–1
INST	1–2	INST	1½–2
FRUST	3+	FRUST	2½+

Comprehension Check

(F)   1. ____   Who were the children in the story?
(Bob and Jane)

(F)   2. ____   What did they see?
(Funny little car)

(I)   3. ____   Who saw the car first?
(Jane)

(F)   4. ____   What was the car called?
(Work car or help car)

(I)   5. ____   These little work cars go between the planes and the terminal building; what do they do?
(Carry baggage or luggage)

Form A Part 2 / *Level P* (33 words)   W.P.M.

‾‾‾‾ / 1980

Background Knowledge Assessment.   Have you ever flown on an airplane? Tell me about it. (If not, what might it be like.)   adequate ☐   inadequate ☐

Jack's First Airplane Ride

Jack and his father got on the airplane.

Away they flew.

"We are up high," said Jack.

"The trees look small."

"And so do the animals," said Father.

Jack said, "This is fun!"

Scoring Guide   Primer

SIG WR Errors		COMP Errors	
IND	0	IND	0–1
INST	1–2	INST	1½–2
FRUST	3+	FRUST	2½+

Comprehension Check

(F)   1. ____   Who was with Jack on the airplane?
(Father)

(F)   2. ____   What words in the story told that Jack liked his ride?
(This is fun!)

(V)   3. ____   What did the word "high" mean in the story?
(Way up in the air, above the buildings, trees, etc.)

(I)   4. ____   What in the story told you that Jack and his father were up high?
(The trees and animals looked small. They were flying.)

(F)   5. ____   How many airplane rides did Jack have before this one?
(None)

---

15. See pp. 12-13 for a discussion of W.P.M.

16. See page 8 for a discussion of Background Knowledge Assessment.

Background Knowledge Assessment. This story is about spiders. What can you tell me about spiders?

adequate ☐   inadequate ☐

Plant Spiders

There are all kinds of spiders.

This black and green one is called a plant spider.

A plant spider has small feet.

All spiders have small feet.

Plant spiders live in nests.

They soon learn to hunt for food and build new

nests.

Scoring Guide   First

SIG WR Errors		COMP Errors	
IND	0	IND	0–1
INST	2	INST	1½–2
FRUST	4+	FRUST	2½+

Comprehension Check

(F) 1. _____ Is there more than one kind of spider?
(Yes—many more)

(F) 2. _____ What two things do plant spiders quickly learn?
(Hunt for food and build new nests)

(F) 3. _____ What color was the spider in this story?
(Black and green)

(F) 4. _____ What did the story say about the spider's feet?
(Small feet, little)

(I) 5. _____ What does this spider probably eat?
(Insects, bugs)

Background Knowledge Assessment. At a rodeo cowboys show their skill with wild horses and bulls. Have you ever seen a rodeo (real, movie, T.V.)? adequate ☐ inadequate ☐

The Rodeo

The people at the rodeo stood up.

They were all waiting for the big ride.

Everyone came to see Bob Hill ride Midnight.

Bob Hill is a top rider.

Midnight is the best horse in the show.

He is big and fast. Midnight is a black horse.

Can Bob Hill ride this great horse?

Comprehension Check

(F) 1. ____ What did the people do?
(Stood up, were waiting, etc.)

(I) 2. ____ The people seemed to be excited, why?
(They wanted to see this great horse and or rider.)

(F) 3. ____ What was the name of the horse?
(Midnight)

(F) 4. ____ What did he (Midnight) look like?
(Big, black, strong, etc.)

(F) 5. ____ Why do you think that Bob Hill was a good rider?
(The story said he was a top rider. He had practice.)

Scoring Guide Second

SIG WR Errors		COMP Errors	
IND	0	IND	0–1
INST	3	INST	1½–2
FRUST	5+	FRUST	2½+

Background Knowledge Assessment. Can you tell me the names of birds you have seen? What things can you tell me about these birds?　　adequate ☐　　inadequate ☐

Smart Birds

Everyone knows that birds like to eat seeds and grain. Birds also like to eat little stones called gravel. Birds have to eat the gravel because they don't have teeth to grind their food. The gravel stays in the bird's gizzard which is something like a stomach. When the bird eats seed, the gravel and the seed grind together. All of the seed is mashed up.

Tame birds must be given gravel. Wild birds find their own gravel on the road sides. Now you can see how smart birds are.

Comprehension Check

(F)　1. _____　Name two things birds like to eat.
(Seeds, grain, gravel stones, sand)

(F)　2. _____　Why do birds have to eat sand or gravel?
(Grind their food)

(V)　3. _____　What does the word "grind" mean?
(Crush, make smaller, etc.)

(I)　4. _____　What do you think would happen to birds that can't get any gravel in their food?
(Probably die, get sick)

(I)　5. _____　Why do birds need a gizzard?
(Don't have teeth, holds gravel)

Scoring Guide　Third

SIG WR Errors		COMP Errors	
IND	2	IND	0–1
INST	5–6	INST	1½–2
FRUST	11	FRUST	2½+

Background Knowledge Assessment. A new sport is called sky diving. Have you ever seen a sky diver in action (T.V., Movies)? Tell me about sky diving.   adequate ☐   inadequate ☐

Sky Diving

An exciting new sport in the world today is sky diving. Sky divers do tricks, make falls, and take interesting pictures. This sport takes you away from your everyday life into a wonderful world you have never known. It is almost like being in a dream. Once out of the airplane, you feel as if you can climb walls or float over mountains.

Sky divers work to develop each of their jumps. Men and women are interested in sky diving. In fact, more people learn to sky dive each year. This relaxing sport is one of man's newest adventures.

Comprehension Check

(F) 1. ____ Tell two things that sky divers do.
(Tricks, make falls, take pictures)

(F) 2. ____ Why is sky diving like being in a dream?
(You float, weightlessness, falling, etc.)

(F) 3. ____ Why would people who have a hard week at their job like this sport?
(Relaxing, new world, away from everyday life.)

(I) 4. ____ Why do sky divers need to use airplanes?
(To jump from them.)

(V) 5. ____ Sky divers "work to develop each jump." What does the word "work" mean in this story?
(Do it many times, practices, learn more about it, improves, etc.)

Scoring Guide   Fourth

SIG WR Errors		COMP Errors	
IND	1–2	IND	0–1
INST	5	INST	1½–2
FRUST	9+	FRUST	2½+

Background Knowledge Assessment. Even fish go to school. This story is about a special school for fish. Can you guess what these fish might learn in this school?   adequate ☐   inadequate ☐

An Underwater School

Scientists wanted to prove that seals had excellent hearing. Blind seals were used in the study. The blind seals were trained to expect food when they heard sounds. The seals quickly learned to hear soft sounds at long distances. Fishermen who splash oars or make noises in water should think about this study.

    The same experts also trained seals to tell the difference between two bell-tones. One bell-tone meant food, two bell-tones meant no food. When the seals made mistakes they were given a light tap. The seals were good learners. They easily learned to tell the difference between the bell-tones.

Comprehension Check

(F) 1. ____ What animals or sea mammals did the experts train?
(Seals)

(I) 2. ____ What should fishermen learn from this study?
(That sound carries in water, that animals can hear in water)

(F) 3. ____ When the seals made mistakes, what happened?
(They were given a light tap.)

(F) 4. ____ What did the seals learn?
(To tell the difference between bell-tones, when to come for food)

(F) 5. ____ What can you say about the seals ability to learn?
(They are good learners. They learn quickly. They are smart.)

Scoring Guide Fifth

SIG WR Errors		COMP Errors	
IND	2	IND	0–1
INST	5	INST	1½–2
FRUST	10	FRUST	2½+

Background Knowledge Assessment. If you have ever been to a zoo you probably saw beavers. Beavers build interesting homes. What can you tell me about a beavers home or about beavers?

adequate ☐   inadequate ☐

A Beaver's Home

A beaver's home, called a lodge, always has a flooded lower room. These homes are built in large ponds or streams. Mud and sticks are the main building materials. One room is built above the water level and another room is located under water. The only way a beaver can get into the house is to submerge and enter through an opening in the flooded room. This room serves two purposes: a storage area and a sanctuary from enemies.

Occasionally the lower room becomes dry because the beaver's dam has been destroyed. This energetic animal has to repair the dam quickly or begin building a new home in another place.

Comprehension Check

(F) 1. ____ What is the name of a beaver's home?
(Lodge)

(F) 2. ____ Where do beavers build their homes?
(Ponds or streams)

(V) 3. ____ What does the word "submerge" mean?
(Go under water, duck under, dive, etc.)

(I) 4. ____ What would happen to a beaver if there wasn't water in a stream?
(Home would dry up, couldn't live, etc.)

(F) 5. ____ How does a flooded lower room help a beaver?
(Storehouse, escape from enemies, helps him get into house)

Scoring Guide Sixth

SIG WR Errors		COMP Errors	
IND	2	IND	0–1
INST	5–6	INST	1½–2
FRUST	11	FRUST	2½+

Background Knowledge Assessment. Bobsledders race down steep, icy mountainslopes. Bobsledding is an Olympic Sport. Can you tell me things about Bobsledding?   adequate ☐   inadequate ☐

The Wildest Run in the World

The Van Hoevenberg bobrun near Lake Placid, New York, is the wildest run in the world. This bobrun is steep, icy, and extremely dangerous. It is almost a mile long and has sixteen sharp curves. High banked walls keep the bobsleds from hurtling off the bobrun.

Bobsleds used in competitive races are carefully designed. The lead person must be a skillful driver and the back person serves as the brakeman.

Most championship races at Lake Placid use four-person sleds. The riders bob back and forth together to make the sled go faster. That's how bobsleds got their name. Championship teams at Lake Placid have reached speeds in excess of ninety miles per hour.

Bobsledding has been an Olympic sport since 1924.

Comprehension Check

(F) 1. ____ How many sharp curves did the bobrun in the story have?
(Sixteen)

(F) 2. ____ What do you call the person on back of the bobsled?
(Brakeman)

(I) 3. ____ What does the lead person do?
(Steers, drives the sled)

(F) 4. ____ According to the story, how did bobsleds get their name?
(The riders bobbed back and forth together.)

(V) 5. ____ What does "hurtling" mean?
(Crash, collide, dash violently)

Scoring Guide   Seventh

SIG WR Errors		COMP Errors	
IND	2	IND	0–1
INST	6	INST	1½–2
FRUST	12	FRUST	2½+

Form A Part 2 / Level 8 (141 words)

Motivation   Amelia Earhart was a courageous pioneer. Read these paragraphs to learn more about this courageous woman.

W.P.M.

$$\overline{}/\,8460$$

Amazing Amelia

Amelia Earhart worked to open up new careers for women. She might easily qualify as an early feminist. When World War I ended, there were still a great many fields closed to women. Despite this, Amelia decided to go to medical school. In 1919 it was very difficult for women to get into medical college. Amelia persisted and did get into medical school. After her first year of school Amelia decided to become a pilot.

After only ten hours of training, this amazing woman set a new world flying record. She flew to a height of over two miles.

Soon after this Amelia and an all male crew made a flight across the Atlantic Ocean. This record-breaking flight took exactly twenty hours and forty minutes.

Until her death in 1937, Amelia continued to challenge many things that were thought to be impossible.

Comprehension Check

(F) 1. _____ Why did Amelia leave medical college?
(To become a pilot, didn't like medical college)

(V) 2. _____ What does "feminist" mean?
(A person who is attempting to provide equal opportunities for women)

(F) 3. _____ How high did Amelia fly when she set a new world record?
(Over two miles)

(V) 4. _____ The word persisted was used. What does "persisted" mean?
(Refuse to give up, to endure, etc.)

(I) 5. _____ What is meant by this statement: "Amelia challenged the impossible"?
(She tried to break the world flying records. She wanted new opportunities for women, etc.)

Scoring Guide   Eighth

SIG WR Errors		COMP Errors	
IND	3	IND	0–1
INST	7	INST	1½–2
FRUST	14	FRUST	2½+

Form A
Part 3 Graded Spelling Survey

1. Pronounce the word.
2. Use the word in a sentence.
3. Pronounce the word again.
4. Ask the student to spell the word.

1

1 some

2 go

3 he

4 mother

5 was

6 in

7 do

8 it

9 can

10 with

2

1 table

2 you

3 bed

4 must

5 have

6 water

7 many

8 five

9 other

10 much

3

1 news

2 things

3 six

4 teacher

5 roof

6 farmer

7 walked

8 ready

9 part

10 carry

4

1 choose

2 witch

3 fit

4 burned

5 forest

6 raise

7 learn

8 given

9 everyone

10 turkey

5

1 delay

2 owner

3 laid

4 seventeen

5 parties

6 study

7 airplane

8 having

9 strike

10 bucket

6

1 central

2 prevent

3 profit

4 serving

5 directly

6 material

7 wherever

8 adventure

9 canvas

10 pleased

Teacher note: Discontinue when the student makes five spelling errors in any one level.

Form B
Part 1 Graded Word Lists

PP		P	
1	far	1	was
2	black	2	play
3	can	3	three
4	to	4	farming
5	and	5	ball
6	at	6	now
7	helps	7	reading
8	some	8	children
9	fast	9	went
10	car	10	then
11	big	11	yellow
12	said	12	barn
13	green	13	trees
14	book	14	red
15	away	15	good
16	see	16	into
17	there	17	that
18	work	18	something
19	is	19	what
20	little	20	saw

1

1 men

2 painted

3 flowers

4 them

5 fire

6 tell

7 her

8 please

9 light

10 cannot

11 eight

12 trucks

13 ground

14 drop

15 stopping

16 from

17 street

18 fireman

19 birthday

20 let's

2

1 sorry

2 climb

3 isn't

4 beautiful

5 wise

6 head

7 cowboy

8 high

9 people

10 nice

11 horn

12 everyone

13 strong

14 I'm

15 room

16 blew

17 gray

18 that's

19 both

20 deer

3

1 hour

2 direction

3 turkeys

4 anything

5 chief

6 foolish

7 enough

8 escape

9 chased

10 magic

11 matter

12 crawl

13 unhappy

14 clothes

15 mind

16 pencil

17 driving

18 discover

19 picture

20 nail

4

1 pedal

2 grateful

3 trail

4 machine

5 ought

6 exercise

7 disturbed

8 force

9 weather

10 properly

11 mountains

12 island

13 defeat

14 guides

15 moan

16 settlers

17 pitching

18 predict

19 west

20 knowledge

5

1 whether

2 concern

3 sharpness

4 pacing

5 shrill

6 freedom

7 loudly

8 expert

9 musical

10 considerable

11 examined

12 remarkably

13 muffled

14 muscle

15 oars

16 delicious

17 octave

18 terrific

19 hymn

20 confusing

6

1 torrent

2 nostrils

3 culprit

4 sensitive

5 calmly

6 tangle

7 wreath

8 teamwork

9 billows

10 knights

11 instinct

12 arrangement

13 pounce

14 rumored

15 strutted

16 demon

17 hearth

18 shifted

19 customers

20 authority

Form B
Part 2 Graded Paragraphs
Designed for Elementary School Children (Grades 1-6)

This is an optional form added to the Classroom Reading Inventory. It may be used in any of the following ways.

1. As an additional set of graded paragraphs for posttesting

2. As a set of silent paragraphs for students who might reject oral reading

3. As a set of silent paragraphs used with Form A

4. As a set of paragraphs for assessing the student's listening capacity level.

The Play Car

"See my play car," said Tom.
"It can go fast."
Ann said, "It's a big car."
"Yes," said Tom.
"Would you like a ride?"

Our Bus Ride

It was time to go to the farm.
"Get in the bus," said Mrs. Brown.
"We are ready to go now."
The children climbed in the bus.
And away went the bus.
It was a good day for a ride.

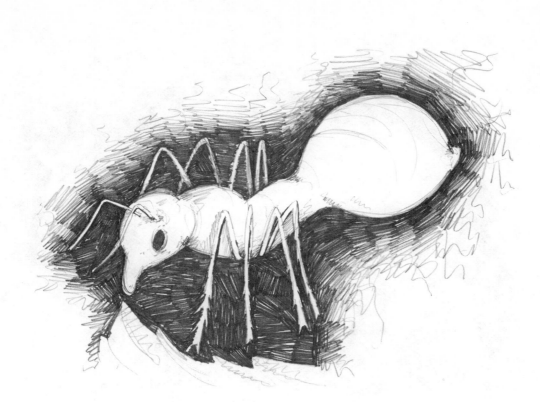

Red Ants

Red ants live in the sand.
They live under the ground.
These ants have many houses.
Each red ant builds its own room.
They must take the sand outside.
The sand is made into little hills.
Ants are busy bugs.

People and Bulls

Before a bull fight some people wait in the streets.
Then angry bulls chase them down the streets.
Some people try to hide.
"Here come the bulls," they yell.
Run for your lives.
Some people get hurt.
Others think it is great fun.

Silly Birds

Even with food all around, turkeys will not eat. Turkeys can really be called "silly birds." Many die from lack of food. Straw is kept in their houses but some never seem to discover what it is used for. We will never understand senseless turkeys.

The silly young birds don't know enough to come out of the cold, either. So many get sick and die. If they see anything bright, they try to eat it. It may be a pencil, a small nail, or even a shovel. You can see how foolish these "silly birds" are.

The Conestoga Wagon

People riding in wagon trains did not have our easy ways of traveling. Their trip was made in what was called a Conestoga wagon. These were good wagons, but they were not comfortable. The wagons were large. They had broad wooden seats. Sitting on these seats was a weary task. The bumping and churning of the ride could be compared to being on a ship in rough water. When this old wagon reached a river, the wheels were removed. Then the wagon was made into a flat boat. These are but a few of the interesting facts about these old wagons.

The Ground Cuckoo

The ground cuckoo is an unusual bird. He is about twenty-four inches long, including his long tail. He also has a long beak and a crested head. You can find him in the Southwestern states.

This bird is helpful to man in many ways. He catches small lizards, insects, and even young rattlesnakes for food. His great speed in running along the ground serves to make this possible.

Some people make a pet of the ground cuckoo. It can be trained to catch mice and other house pests.

You may know this bird by another name. It is also called a road runner.

Blaze: Rebel Horse

All the ranchers in the valley knew about the wild stallion named Blaze, a powerful horse with a red mane. Many of the local men tried to catch this rebel but failed each time. A reward was offered for his capture—dead or alive, because he encouraged other horses to run away with him.

Pete Cook and six other men were determined to catch Blaze. Pete used binoculars to study the wild horse's movements. He made several maps of the valley and was sure he could capture Blaze this time.

Pete posted the men all along the secluded trails that Blaze usually followed. Each rider would pick up Blaze along the trail and force him into a narrow canyon, where Pete would be waiting.

The men succeeded in forcing Blaze into the narrow canyon. Pete was ready with his rope but Blaze came at him in a wild rage. Pete lost his balance but was able to roll over out of the way. Blaze saw his chance to escape and got away once again.

Salt Flat Speed

Rolling up to the starting line at Utah's Bonneville Salt Flats was a racing car that looked like something designed by Dr. Frankenstein on his day off. It had "Green Monster" emblazoned on its side. It was so ugly that some called it "the garbage truck." Over the huge jet intake on its nose was a short wing that looked like a coffee table. Bulging from its side was a cockpit in which the driver steered the car lying almost flat. But the Green Monster soon demonstrated that it was no truck.

Howling like a banshee, it streaked through the measured mile at 396 miles per hour. Then it turned around and sped back through the mile once more. This time the speed was 479 miles per hour. U.S. Auto Club officials checked their electronic timers and averaged the two runs. Art Arfons, the Green Monster's builder and driver, had set a new world's land-speed mark of 437.5 miles per hour! Racing cars now travel over 600 MPH.

So Throw the Ball

One day recently when my wife turned on our television set to a Yankee-White Sox game, I noticed a phenomenon that intrigued me greatly. I happened to have the New York Times on my lap. When the catcher threw the ball back to Jim Brosnan, the Sox pitcher, I discovered that I could safely look away from the television screen, read a couple of paragraphs in the Times, and still revert my eyes in time for the pitch.

Subsequently I have begun timing baseball games with a stopwatch. I can only conclude that the modern pitcher hates to pitch. He cannot bear the thought of throwing the ball toward the plate. His ingenuity at postponing the fateful moment is uncanny. In the fastest game I have observed recently, the pitchers on the two teams held the ball for a total of one hour, eight minutes, and thirty seconds!

Form B

Form B is an optional form added to the Classroom Reading Inventory. It may be used in any of the following ways.

1. As an additional set of graded paragraphs for posttesting

2. As a set of silent paragraphs for students who might reject oral reading

3. As a set of silent paragraphs to enable the teacher to give an oral paragraph and a corresponding silent paragraph for a more complete assessment of the student's overall reading achievement

4. As a set of paragraphs for assessing the student's listening capacity level (See p. 8)

Form B Inventory Record ──────────────

Summary Sheet

Student's Name _____ Grade _____ Age (Chronological) _____

Date _____ School _____ Administered by _____

yrs. mos.

Part 1 Word Lists			Part 2 Graded Paragraphs			
Grade Level	Percent of Words Correct	Word Recognition Errors		SIG WR	Comp	L.C.

Part 1 — Word Lists:

Grade Level	Percent of Words Correct
PP	_____
1 P	_____
1	_____
2	_____
3	_____
4	_____
5	_____
6	_____

Word Recognition Errors

Consonants
- ____ Consonants
- ____ blends
- ____ digraphs
- ____ endings
- ____ compounds
- ____ contractions

Vowels
- ____ long
- ____ short
- ____ long/short oo
- ____ vowel + r
- ____ diphthong
- ____ vowel comb.
- ____ a + 1 or w

Syllable
- ____ visual patterns
- ____ prefix
- ____ suffix

Word Recognition
reinforcement and
Vocabulary
development

Part 2 — Graded Paragraphs:

	SIG WR	Comp	L.C.
PP			
P			
1			
2			
3			
4			
5			
6			
7			
8			

Estimated Levels

	Grade
Independent	_____
Instructional	_____ (range)
Frustration	_____
Listening Capacity	_____

Comp Errors

- _____ Factual (F)
- _____ Inference (I)
- _____ Vocabulary (V)
- _____ "Word Caller"
  (A student who
  reads without asso-
  ciating meaning)
- _____ Poor Memory

Summary of Specific Needs:

PP		P		1		2	
1 far	_____	1 was	_____	1 men	_____	1 sorry	_____
2 black	_____	2 play	_____	2 painted	_____	2 climb	_____
3 can	_____	3 three	_____	3 flowers	_____	3 isn't	_____
4 to	_____	4 farming	_____	4 them	_____	4 beautiful	_____
5 and	_____	5 ball	_____	5 fire	_____	5 wise	_____
6 at	_____	6 now	_____	6 tell	_____	6 head	_____
7 helps	_____	7 reading	_____	7 her	_____	7 cowboy	_____
8 some	_____	8 children	_____	8 please	_____	8 high	_____
9 fast	_____	9 went	_____	9 light	_____	9 people	_____
10 car	_____	10 then	_____	10 cannot	_____	10 nice	_____
11 big	_____	11 yellow	_____	11 eight	_____	11 horn	_____
12 said	_____	12 barn	_____	12 trucks	_____	12 everyone	_____
13 green	_____	13 trees	_____	13 ground	_____	13 strong	_____
14 book	_____	14 red	_____	14 drop	_____	14 I'm	_____
15 away	_____	15 good	_____	15 stopping	_____	15 room	_____
16 see	_____	16 into	_____	16 from	_____	16 blew	_____
17 there	_____	17 that	_____	17 street	_____	17 gray	_____
18 work	_____	18 something	_____	18 fireman	_____	18 that's	_____
19 is	_____	19 what	_____	19 birthday	_____	19 both	_____
20 little	_____	20 saw	_____	20 let's	_____	20 deer	_____
	_____ %		_____ %		_____ %		_____ %

Teacher note: If the child missed five words in any column—stop Part 1. Begin Graded Paragraphs, Part 2, (Form B), at highest level in which child recognized all 20 words. To save time, if the first ten words were correct, go on to the next list. If one of the first ten words were missed, continue the entire list.

Form B Part 1

3		4		5		6	
1 hour	_____	1 pedal	_____	1 whether	_____	1 torrent	_____
2 direction	_____	2 grateful	_____	2 concern	_____	2 nostrils	_____
3 turkeys	_____	3 trail	_____	3 sharpness	_____	3 culprit	_____
4 anything	_____	4 machine	_____	4 pacing	_____	4 sensitive	_____
5 chief	_____	5 ought	_____	5 shrill	_____	5 calmly	_____
6 foolish	_____	6 exercise	_____	6 freedom	_____	6 tangle	_____
7 enough	_____	7 disturbed	_____	7 loudly	_____	7 wreath	_____
8 escape	_____	8 force	_____	8 expert	_____	8 teamwork	_____
9 chased	_____	9 weather	_____	9 musical	_____	9 billows	_____
10 magic	_____	10 properly	_____	10 considerable	_____	10 knights	_____
11 matter	_____	11 mountains	_____	11 examined	_____	11 instinct	_____
12 crawl	_____	12 island	_____	12 remarkably	_____	12 arrangement	_____
13 unhappy	_____	13 defeat	_____	13 muffled	_____	13 pounce	_____
14 clothes	_____	14 guides	_____	14 muscle	_____	14 rumored	_____
15 mind	_____	15 moan	_____	15 oars	_____	15 strutted	_____
16 pencil	_____	16 settlers	_____	16 delicious	_____	16 demon	_____
17 driving	_____	17 pitching	_____	17 octave	_____	17 hearth	_____
18 discover	_____	18 predict	_____	18 terrific	_____	18 shifted	_____
19 picture	_____	19 west	_____	19 hymn	_____	19 customers	_____
20 nail	_____	20 knowledge	_____	20 confusing	_____	20 authority	_____
	_____ %		_____ %		_____ %		_____ %

Form B Part 2 / *Level PP* **(24 words)**

Background Knowledge Assessment. This story is about two children and their play car. Tell what you think the children are doing?[17]   adequate ☐   inadequate ☐

The Play Car

"See my play car," said Tom.

"It can go fast."

Ann said, "It's a big car."

"Yes," said Tom.

"Would you like a ride?"

Scoring Guide Preprimer

SIG WR Errors		COMP Errors	
IND	0	IND	0–1
INST	1–2	INST	1½–2
FRUST	3+	FRUST	2½+

Comprehension Check

(F) 1. ____ What are the names of the boy and girl in the story?
(Tom and Ann)

(F) 2. ____ What were they talking about?
(The play car, etc.)

(F) 3. ____ Who owned the car?
(Tom)

(F) 4. ____ What did Ann (the girl) say about the car?
(Big car)

(I) 5. ____ Tell one thing that Tom might have liked about the car.
(It was fast, big.)

Form B Part 2 / *Level P* **(40 words)**

Background Knowledge Assessment. Has your class ever taken a field trip? What can you tell about field trips?   adequate ☐   inadequate ☐

Our Bus Ride

It was time to go to the farm.

"Get in the bus," said Mrs. Brown.

"We are ready to go now."

The children climbed in the bus.

And away went the bus.

It was a good day for a ride.

Scoring Guide Primer

SIG WR Errors		COMP Errors	
IND	0	IND	0–1
INST	2	INST	1½–2
FRUST	4+	FRUST	2½+

Comprehension Check

(F) 1. ____ Where were they going?
(Farm)

(F) 2. ____ How were they going?
(By bus)

(I) 3. ____ Who was Mrs. Brown?
(Teacher, or bus driver)

(F) 4. ____ How did the children know that it was time for the bus to leave?
(Mrs. Brown said, "We are ready to go now.")

(F) 5. ____ Was this bus ride taking place during the day or at night?
(Day)

---

17. See page 8 for a discussion of Background Knowledge Assessment.

Background Knowledge Assessment. Red ants live underground. What do you think it would be like to live in an underground home?   adequate ☐   inadequate ☐

Red Ants

Red ants live in the sand.

They live under the ground.

These ants have many houses.

Each red ant builds its own room.

They must take the sand outside.

The sand is made into little hills.

Ants are busy bugs.

Scoring Guide   First

SIG WR Errors		COMP Errors	
IND	0	IND	0–1
INST	2	INST	1½–2
FRUST	4+	FRUST	2½+

Comprehension Check

(F) 1. _____ Where do the ants in this story build their homes?
(Underground, in sand, everywhere)

(F) 2. _____ How many houses do ants have?
(Many, lots, several)

(I) 3. _____ Why do ants have to take sand outside?
(Because there is no room in the holes underground)

(V) 4. _____ What did the word "busy" mean in the story?
(Hard workers, working all of the time, etc.)

(F) 5. _____ What color were the ants in this story?
(Red)

W.P.M.

_____/2580

Background Knowledge Assessment. Can you imagine mean bulls loose in a crowd of people? What might happen?   adequate ☐   inadequate ☐

People and Bulls

Before a bull fight some people wait in the streets.

Then angry bulls chase them down the streets.

Some people try to hide.

"Here come the bulls," they yell.

Run for your lives.

Some people get hurt.

Others think it is great fun.

Scoring Guide Second

SIG WR Errors		COMP Errors	
IND	0	IND	0–1
INST	3	INST	1½–2
FRUST	5+	FRUST	2½+

Comprehension Check

(F) 1. ____ Why did the people run from the bulls?
(Because the bulls might hurt them)

(F) 2. ____ What did the people do just before the big bull fight?
(Waited in the streets)

(I) 3. ____ Some people hid but others waited for the bulls. Why?
(See if they could get away from the bulls or challenge the bulls)

(I) 4. ____ What made the bulls angry?
(People teased them, they were frightened, etc.)

(V) 5. ____ What does the word "chase" mean?
(To run after, etc.)

Background Knowledge Assessment. Baby turkeys do unusual things. What unusual things do you think they do? adequate ☐ inadequate ☐

Silly Birds

Even with food all around, turkeys will not eat. Turkeys can really be called "silly birds." Many die from lack of food. Straw is kept in their houses but some never seem to discover what it is used for. We will never understand senseless turkeys.

    The silly young birds don't know enough to come out of the cold, either. So many get sick and die. If they see anything bright, they try to eat it. It may be a pencil, a small nail, or even a shovel. You can see how foolish these "silly birds" are.

Comprehension Check

(F) 1. _____ This story tells about young or old turkeys?
(Young)

(F) 2. _____ What do turkeys do when they see something bright?
(Try to eat it)

(I) 3. _____ What happens to turkeys that do silly things?
(They die)

(F) 4. _____ Tell at least two things that a baby turkey will try to eat.
(Pencil, nail, shovel, or something bright)

(I) 5. _____ What do you think was the most important thing this story told you about turkeys?
(They are very foolish, silly, or dumb)

Scoring Guide Third

SIG WR Errors		COMP Errors	
IND	2	IND	0–1
INST	5	INST	1½–2
FRUST	10	FRUST	2½+

Background Knowledge Assessment. Long before you were born people traveled in covered wagons called Conestoga Wagons. Conestoga wagons are shown on TV and in movies. Can you tell things about such a wagon or how people traveled long ago?

adequate ☐   inadequate ☐

The Conestoga Wagon

People riding in wagon trains did not have our easy ways of traveling. Their trip was made in what was called a Conestoga wagon. These were good wagons, but they were not comfortable. The wagons were large. They had broad wooden seats. Sitting on these seats was a weary task. The bumping and churning of the ride could be compared to being on a ship in rough water. When this old wagon reached a river, the wheels were removed. Then the wagon was made into a flat boat. These are but a few of the interesting facts about these old wagons.

Comprehension Check

(F) 1. ____ What made riding in a Conestoga wagon unpleasant?
(Bumps, sitting on wooden seats, etc.)

(F) 2. ____ According to the story, "riding on a wagon was like what other type of ride?"
(Like being on a ship in rough water)

(I) 3. ____ Traveling by Conestoga wagon was one important way for people to travel. True or False?
(True)

(F) 4. ____ How did the people get the wagon across deep streams?
(Used the wagon as a flat boat by taking off the wheels)

(V) 5. ____ What does the word "weary" mean?
(Tired, uncomfortable, etc.)

Scoring Guide   Fourth

SIG WR Errors		COMP Errors	
IND	2	IND	0–1
INST	5	INST	1½–2
FRUST	10	FRUST	2½+

W.P.M.

___ / 6060

Background Knowledge Assessment. When you read this story you will learn that the name Ground Cuckoo is a special name for a popular bird. What things can you tell about birds?

adequate ☐   inadequate ☐

The Ground Cuckoo

The ground cuckoo is an unusual bird. He is about twenty-four inches long, including his long tail. He also has a long beak and a crested head. You can find him in the southwestern States.

This bird is helpful to man in many ways. He catches small lizards, insects, and even young rattlesnakes for food. His great speed in running along the ground serves to make this possible.

Some people make a pet of the ground cuckoo. It can be trained to catch mice and other house pests.

You may know this bird by another name. It is also called a roadrunner.

Comprehension Check

(F) 1. _____ How is the ground cuckoo helpful to man?
(Catches insects, pets, snakes, etc.)

(F) 2. _____ Where is the ground cuckoo found?
(In Southwestern U.S.)

(I) 3. _____ What is unusual about the ground cuckoo?
(Speed, funny looking, etc.)

(F) 4. _____ Describe the ground cuckoo.
(twenty-four inches long, crested head, long beak, fast runner, etc.)

(F) 5. _____ What is another name for the ground cuckoo?
(Roadrunner)

Scoring Guide   Fifth

SIG WR Errors		COMP Errors	
IND	2	IND	0–1
INST	5	INST	1½–2
FRUST	10	FRUST	2½+

Background Knowledge Assessment. This story tells about how a group of men attempted to capture a wild horse. What are some things these men would have to do to capture this wild horse?

adequate ☐   inadequate ☐

Blaze: Rebel Horse

All the ranchers in the valley knew about the wild stallion named Blaze, a powerful horse with a red mane. Many of the local men tried to catch this rebel but failed each time. A reward was offered for his capture—dead or alive, because he encouraged other horses to run away with him.

Pete Cook and six other men were determined to catch Blaze. Pete used binoculars to study the wild horse's movements. He made several maps of the valley and was sure he could capture Blaze this time.

Pete posted the men all along the secluded trails that Blaze usually followed. Each rider would pick up Blaze along the trail and force him into a narrow canyon, where Pete would be waiting.

The men succeeded in forcing Blaze into the narrow canyon. Pete was ready with his rope but Blaze came at him in a wild rage. Pete lost his balance but was able to roll over out of the way. Blaze saw his chance to escape and got away once again.

Comprehension Check

(F) 1. _____ Why did the ranchers want the wild horse (Blaze) captured?
(He encouraged other horses to run away.)

(F) 2. _____ What did the wild horse (Blaze) look like?
(Powerful, big, red mane)

(F) 3. _____ What did Pete Cook do before attempting to capture Blaze?
(He made maps of the valley and of the horse's trails.)

(V) 4. _____ What does "secluded" mean?
(Hidden, secret, hard to find)

(I) 5. _____ Describe how Pete's men worked as a team to capture Blaze.
(They spread out and forced him into a narrow canyon.)

Scoring Guide Sixth

SIG WR Errors		COMP Errors	
IND	0–3	IND	0–1
INST	8	INST	1½–2
FRUST	17	FRUST	2½+

Background Knowledge Assessment. Fast cars are interesting to some people. Highways are designed to allow cars to travel at 55 miles per hour. Imagine a car that traveled faster than 600 mph.

adequate ☐   inadequate ☐

Salt Flat Speed

Rolling up to the starting line at Utah's Bonneville Salt Flats was a racing car that looked like something designed by Dr. Frankenstein on his day off. It had "Green Monster" emblazoned on its side. It was so ugly that some called it "the garbage truck." Over the huge jet intake on its nose was a short wing that looked like a coffee table. Bulging from its side was a cockpit in which the driver steered the car lying almost flat. But the Green Monster soon demonstrated that it was no truck.

Howling like a banshee, it streaked through the measured mile at 396 miles per hour. Then it turned around and sped back through the mile once more. This time the speed was 479 miles per hour. U.S. Auto Club officials checked their electronic timers and averaged the two runs. Art Arfons, the Green Monster's builder and driver, had set a new world's land-speed mark of 437.5 miles per hour! Racing cars now travel over 600 MPH.

Comprehension Check

(F) 1. ____ What was the name of this car?
(Green Monster)

(F) 2. ____ Why did some people call this car a "garbage truck"?
(Because it was ugly, because they didn't think it could set a record)

(F) 3. ____ What did the race car have over its jet intake on the nose of the car?
(A short wing)

(V) 4. ____ The words "howled like a banshee" were used in this selection, what does that mean?
(A wailing, screeching, eerie, noise)

(I) 5. ____ Why won't we see the Green Monster or a car like it driving along our streets?
(Car is too fast)

Scoring Guide   Seventh

SIG WR Errors		COMP Errors	
IND	3	IND	0–1
INST	7–8	INST	1½–2
FRUST	15	FRUST	2½+

Background Knowledge Assessment. The author has a specific attitude regarding baseball pitchers. Can you guess about the authors attitude? adequate ☐ inadequate ☐

So Throw the Ball

One day recently when my wife turned on our television set to a Yankee-White Sox game, I noticed a phenomenon that intrigued me greatly. I happened to have the New York Times on my lap. When the catcher threw the ball back to Jim Brosnan, the Sox pitcher, I discovered that I could safely look away from the television screen, read a couple of paragraphs in the Times, and still revert my eyes in time for the pitch.

Subsequently I have begun timing baseball games with a stopwatch. I can only conclude that the modern pitcher hates to pitch. He cannot bear the thought of throwing the ball toward the plate. His ingenuity at postponing the fateful moment is uncanny. In the fastest game I have observed recently, the pitchers on the two teams held the ball for a total of one hour, eight minutes, and thirty seconds!

Comprehension Check

(F) 1. ____ Name the teams mentioned in the story?
(Yankees and White Sox)

(F) 2. ____ What paper was the man reading?
(New York Times)

(I) 3. ____ How did the author feel about the pitcher holding the ball so long?
(He felt it was unnecessary.)

(V) 4. ____ What does "ingenious" mean?
(Clever, original, smart, etc.)

(V) 5. ____ What does "revert" mean?
(To go back, return, etc.)

Scoring Guide Eighth

SIG WR Errors		COMP Errors	
IND	3	IND	0–1
INST	7–8	INST	1½–2
FRUST	15	FRUST	2½+

Form B
Part 3 Graded Spelling Survey

Form B Part 3/Spelling Survey

1. Pronounce the word.
2. Use the word in a sentence.
3. Pronounce the word again.
4. Ask the student to spell the word.

1	2	3
1 on	1 here	1 place
2 like	2 pull	2 laughing
3 see	3 was	3 wall
4 have	4 cry	4 reason
5 we	5 man	5 holding
6 at	6 more	6 sitting
7 of	7 men	7 walking
8 big	8 eye	8 early
9 a	9 her	9 Mrs.
10 me	10 hops	10 watched

4	5	6
1 cost	1 pride	1 we're
2 below	2 level	2 burden
3 marks	3 candle	3 bushel
4 belong	4 claim	4 shipment
5 sometime	5 feather	5 purchase
6 raised	6 taste	6 illness
7 eight	7 pleasure	7 jewel
8 bathing	8 neighbor	8 manager
9 field	9 waste	9 active
10 leaders	10 island	10 precious

Teacher note: Discontinue when the student makes five spelling errors in any one level.

Form C

Part 1 Grade Word Lists
Designed for Junior High School Students

1

1 men

2 nailed

3 found

4 then

5 four

6 told

7 him

8 place

9 night

10 another

11 freight

12 clock

13 garbage

14 dress

15 grow

16 frog

17 struck

18 birthday

19 peanut

20 don't

2

1 slide

2 clang

3 I'll

4 beauty

5 wheels

6 hand

7 chipmunk

8 right

9 pencil

10 twice

11 torn

12 together

13 strange

14 dollars

15 boats

16 blow

17 great

18 there's

19 mouth

20 mail

3

1 soup

2 breath

3 remember

4 afternoon

5 chief

6 choose

7 enough

8 enemy

9 cheese

10 dessert

11 inventor

12 cousin

13 unusual

14 clothing

15 drown

16 plate

17 scent

18 disappointed

19 posture

20 pale

4

1 barrel

2 awkward

3 trial

4 nephew

5 fought

6 experience

7 dispose

8 cowards

9 wheat

10 trousers

11 mounted

12 iron

13 legends

14 ghost

15 groan

16 servants

17 pitcher

18 perched

19 weight

20 knowledge

5

1 whether

2 notched

3 sandals

4 pronged

5 squaws

6 shrill

7 length

8 contest

9 muscle

10 chant

11 excused

12 vinegar

13 shuffled

14 pierce

15 bore

16 delicious

17 orchard

18 territory

19 pouches

20 plateau

6

1 moisture

2 dorsal

3 contrary

4 sausage

5 notions

6 pounce

7 envelope

8 request

9 wreath

10 knights

11 irregular

12 torrent

13 salad

14 applause

15 hustling

16 tenor

17 hearth

18 surf

19 condition

20 official

7

1 numberless

2 derby

3 omen

4 rayon

5 accumulate

6 dense

7 potential

8 terrain

9 vivid

10 segment

11 amber

12 humidity

13 monarch

14 publication

15 meteorite

16 ridicule

17 domestic

18 focus

19 irregular

20 algebra

8

1 pulverize

2 custody

3 delusion

4 barbarian

5 privacy

6 embankment

7 designate

8 notorious

9 arrogant

10 quote

11 variation

12 pneumonia

13 embassy

14 yacht

15 authentic

16 brigade

17 browse

18 recruit

19 motive

20 belligerent

Form C

Part 2 Graded Paragraphs
Designed for Junior High School Students

Grasshoppers

Grasshoppers come from eggs. They have four long wings and six legs. Some grasshoppers live on the ground; others live in trees. All grasshoppers can jump and fly. They fly high in the air. They jump, fly, and play. Most grasshoppers are green, black, or brown.

The John F. Kennedy Space Center

A ball of fire is seen in the sky. The sky turns red and orange. Another rocket has been tested! Most rocket tests are made in Florida. The first test was made in 1958. In 1969 men were sent to the moon. People near the space center see rockets going off all the time. Almost every day is like the Fourth of July. We do not shoot them just for fun. We hope to learn things about space.

Yellowstone National Park

Each year more than two million people visit Yellowstone National Park. It is the largest of our national parks. The park is more than 8,000 feet above sea level. It has many natural hot water fountains called geysers. "Old Faithful" is the best-known of the geysers. It is not the largest, but is famous because it is so regular in its activity. "Old Faithful" shoots water and steam over 120 feet in the air. It does this about every 73 minutes, summer and winter. It has been doing this since early times! You can see why so many people visit this great park.

A Great American Sport

The history of baseball shows that the game has changed a great deal since it was first played. In 1839, Abner Doubleday set up the rules for playing a baseball game.

Later on, uniforms appeared. The players wore long pants, a fancy white shirt, and a straw hat. The umpire wore a long coat, a tall silk hat, and carried a cane. Rakes, ax handles, and tree branches were used as bats.

The first World Series was played in 1903. Baseball fans wanted to see the top teams from the two major leagues play. The winners would be the champions of the baseball world.

Driver Education

Even our parents may have some bad driving habits. This is why young drivers should take lessons from trained teachers.

A recent story makes this point. A young driver had learned from an older one. While driving, a young driver felt his two right wheels go off the road. He yanked the car quickly back onto the road. As a result, the car turned over. A passenger in the car was killed. A trained teacher would have taught the driver not to slam on the brakes. And not to turn back onto the road too quickly.

One of the best ways to decrease traffic accidents is to have more driver education.

Sentinels in the Forest

Many wild creatures that travel with their own kind know by instinct how to protect the group. One of them acts as a sentinel.

Hidden by the branches of a low-hanging tree, I once watched two white-tailed deer feeding in a meadow. At first, my interest was held by their beauty. But soon I noticed something which was quite unusual; they were taking turns at feeding.

One deer was calmly cropping grass, unafraid and at ease. The other, a sentinel, stood guard against enemies. The guard deer watched every movement and used its sensitive nostrils to "feel" the air. Not for a moment, during the half hour I spied upon them, did they stop their teamwork.

Modern Airports

In the earliest days of aviation, there was no need for airports. The light wood-and-cloth airplanes could take off and land in any level, open field.

In contrast to these simple airfields, the modern airport is almost a city in itself. There are many buildings and services for the convenience and comfort of the passengers.

Waiting rooms, restaurants, barbershops, post offices, banks, souvenir shops, florists, and even bowling alleys are likely to be located at the airport.

But the heart of the airport is still the area where the planes take off and land—the runways. Jet planes require very long runways—sometimes as much as two miles in length. Runways are paved with concrete to withstand the impact of planes weighing over 375 tons hitting the ground at speeds between 110 and 140 miles per hour. Taxiways link the runways with each other and with terminal buildings.

Sports Cars

To most laymen, a sports car is simply a vehicle with a flashy, streamlined body decorated with plenty of chrome. Such a vehicle, however, might easily be everything that an actual sports car should not be. It is the engineering features that the untrained eye does not observe which distinguish the true sports car from the bloated, over-chromed and highly colored dream cars that cruise along the American freeways on weekend afternoons.

The meticulously engineered features of a genuine sports car are those observed on the road rather than those idolized in the parking lots of country clubs. That which ordinarily is referred to as an American sports car would not be permitted to enter a European road race, because it would be too unsafe both for its own operator and for the other participants in a race. For another thing, it would be ridiculously outclassed for acceleration and roadability under conditions of such competitive driving.

Form C

Form C may be used in any of the following ways.

1. As a set of *silent paragraphs* for students who might reject oral reading

2. As a set of *silent paragraphs* used with Form D

3. As a set of *paragraphs* for assessing the student's listening capacity level. (see p. 8)

Summary Sheet

Student's Name _____ Grade _____ Age (Chronological) _____

yrs. mos.

Date _____ School _____ Administered by _____

Part 1 Word Lists			Part 2 Graded Paragraphs		
Grade Level	Percent of Words Correct	Word Recognition Errors		SIG WR	Comp	L.C.

Grade Level	Percent of Words Correct	Word Recognition Errors		SIG WR	Comp	L.C.
1	_____	Consonants	PP			
		____ Consonants	P			
		____ blends	1			
		____ digraphs	2			
		____ endings	3			
		____ compounds	4			
		____ contractions	5			
2	_____	Vowels	6			
		____ long	7			
		____ short	8			
		____ long/short oo				
		____ vowel + r				
		____ diphthong				
		____ vowel comb.				
		____ a + 1 or w				

Estimated Levels

	Grade
Independent	_____
Instructional	_____ (range)
Frustration	_____
Listening Capacity	_____

Grade Level	Percent of Words Correct	Word Recognition Errors
3	_____	Syllable
4	_____	____ visual patterns
5	_____	____ prefix
6	_____	____ suffix
7	_____	Word Recognition reinforcement and Vocabulary development
8	_____	

Comp Errors

_____ Factual (F)

_____ Inference (I)

_____ Vocabulary (V)

_____ "Word Caller"
     (A student who
     reads without asso-
     ciating meaning)

_____ Poor Memory

Summary of Specific Needs:

Form C Part 1/Graded Word Lists

1		**2**		**3**		**4**	
1 men	_____	1 slide	_____	1 soup	_____	1 barrel	_____
2 nailed	_____	2 clang	_____	2 breath	_____	2 awkward	_____
3 found	_____	3 I'll	_____	3 remember	_____	3 trial	_____
4 then	_____	4 beauty	_____	4 afternoon	_____	4 nephew	_____
5 four	_____	5 wheels	_____	5 chief	_____	5 fought	_____
6 told	_____	6 hand	_____	6 choose	_____	6 experience	_____
7 him	_____	7 chipmunk	_____	7 enough	_____	7 dispose	_____
8 place	_____	8 right	_____	8 enemy	_____	8 cowards	_____
9 night	_____	9 pencil	_____	9 cheese	_____	9 wheat	_____
10 another	_____	10 twice	_____	10 dessert	_____	10 trousers	_____
11 freight	_____	11 torn	_____	11 inventor	_____	11 mounted	_____
12 clock	_____	12 together	_____	12 cousin	_____	12 iron	_____
13 garbage	_____	13 strange	_____	13 unusual	_____	13 legends	_____
14 dress	_____	14 dollars	_____	14 clothing	_____	14 ghost	_____
15 grow	_____	15 boats	_____	15 drown	_____	15 groan	_____
16 frog	_____	16 blow	_____	16 plate	_____	16 servants	_____
17 struck	_____	17 great	_____	17 scent	_____	17 pitcher	_____
18 birthday	_____	18 there's	_____	18 disappointed	_____	18 perched	_____
19 peanut	_____	19 mouth	_____	19 posture	_____	19 weight	_____
20 don't	_____	20 mail	_____	20 pale	_____	20 knowledge	_____
	_____ %		_____ %		_____ %		_____ %

Teacher note: If the student missed five words in any column—stop Part 1. Begin Graded Paragraphs, Part 2, (Form C), at highest level in which all 20 words were recognized. To save time, if the first ten words were correct, go on to the next list. If one of the first ten words were missed, continue the entire list.

Form C Part 1

5		6		7		8	
1 whether	_____	1 moisture	_____	1 numberless	_____	1 pulverized	_____
2 notched	_____	2 dorsal	_____	2 derby	_____	2 custody	_____
3 sandals	_____	3 contrary	_____	3 omen	_____	3 delusion	_____
4 pronged	_____	4 sausage	_____	4 rayon	_____	4 barbarian	_____
5 squaws	_____	5 notions	_____	5 accumulate	_____	5 privacy	_____
6 shrill	_____	6 pounce	_____	6 dense	_____	6 embankment	_____
7 length	_____	7 envelope	_____	7 potential	_____	7 designate	_____
8 contest	_____	8 request	_____	8 terrain	_____	8 notorious	_____
9 muscle	_____	9 wreath	_____	9 vivid	_____	9 arrogant	_____
10 chant	_____	10 knights	_____	10 segment	_____	10 quote	_____
11 excused	_____	11 irregular	_____	11 amber	_____	11 variation	_____
12 vinegar	_____	12 torrent	_____	12 humidity	_____	12 pneumonia	_____
13 shuffled	_____	13 salad	_____	13 monarch	_____	13 embassy	_____
14 pierce	_____	14 applause	_____	14 publication	_____	14 yacht	_____
15 bore	_____	15 hustling	_____	15 meteorite	_____	15 authentic	_____
16 delicious	_____	16 tenor	_____	16 ridicule	_____	16 brigade	_____
17 orchard	_____	17 hearth	_____	17 domestic	_____	17 browse	_____
18 territory	_____	18 surf	_____	18 focus	_____	18 recruit	_____
19 pouches	_____	19 condition	_____	19 irregular	_____	19 motive	_____
20 plateau	_____	20 official	_____	20 algebra	_____	20 belligerent	_____
	_____ %		_____ %		_____ %		_____ %

Background Knowledge Assessment.   What can you tell me about grasshoppers?[18]

adequate ☐   inadequate ☐

Grasshoppers

Grasshoppers come from eggs.

They have four long wings and six legs.

Some grasshoppers live on the ground, others live in

trees.

All grasshoppers can jump and fly.

They fly high in the air.

They jump, fly, and play.

Most grasshoppers are green, black, or brown.

Comprehension Check

(F)   1. ____   How many legs do grasshoppers have?
(Six)

(F)   2. ____   Where do grasshoppers come from?
(Eggs)

(F)   3. ____   Not all grasshoppers are the same color.
Name two colors for them.
(Green, black, or brown)

(F)   4. ____   Name two things that grasshoppers do.
(Fly, jump, play, etc.)

(I)   5. ____   Where are some places that grasshoppers
can hide?
(Grass, weeds or trees difficult to reach)

Scoring Guide   First

SIG WR Errors		COMP Errors	
IND	0	IND	0–1
INST	2	INST	1½–2
FRUST	5	FRUST	2½+

18. See page 8 for a discussion of Background Knowledge Assessment.

Background Knowledge Assessment.   Much has been told about astronauts and the John F. Kennedy Space Center. Tell me things you remember.   adequate ☐   inadequate ☐

The John F. Kennedy Space Center

A ball of fire is seen in the sky. The sky turns red

and orange.

Another rocket has been tested!

Most rocket tests are made in Florida.

The first test was made in 1958.

In 1969 men were sent to the moon.

People near the space center see

rockets going off all the time.

Almost every day is like the Fourth of July. We do

not shoot them just for fun.

We hope to learn things about space.

Comprehension Check

(F)   1. ____   Why do we send rockets into space?
(Learn things about space)

(F)   2. ____   The story said that the sky turns color when rockets are tested, name one.
(Red or orange)

(F)   3. ____   How often do people see the rockets going off?
(All of the time)

(F)   4. ____   The story said that most tests were made in what state?
(Florida)

(I)   5. ____   Rocket testing is like the Fourth of July, why?
(People shoot firecrackers and sky rockets on the 4th)

Scoring Guide   Second

SIG WR Errors		COMP Errors	
IND	1	IND	0–1
INST	3–4	INST	1½–2
FRUST	6	FRUST	2½+

W.P.M.

___/6180

Background Knowledge Assessment. Have you visited a National Park? (If yes, tell about it.) (If no, can you guess what these parks are like?)   adequate ☐   inadequate ☐

Yellowstone National Park

Each year more than two million people visit Yellowstone National Park.

It is the largest of our national parks.

The park is more than 8,000 feet above sea level.

It has many natural hot water fountains called geysers. "Old Faithful" is the best-known of the geysers. It is not the largest, but is famous because it is so regular in its activity. "Old Faithful" shoots water and steam over 120 feet in the air. It does this about every 73 minutes, summer and winter. It has been doing this since early times. You can see why so many people visit this great park.

Comprehension Check

(F)   1. ____ How many people visit Yellowstone National Park each year?
(Over two million)

(F)   2. ____ What is the name of one of the park's famous geysers?
(Old Faithful)

(F)   3. ____ What is a geyser?
(Deep hole in ground water and steam shoot up from it)

(F)   4. ____ Water and steam shoots out of Old Faithful (geyser in this story) how often?
(About every 73 min.)

(I)   5. ____ Why is "Old Faithful's" name a good one?
(It is regular in its activity, summer and winter)

Scoring Guide   Third

SIG WR Errors		COMP Errors	
IND	2	IND	0–1
INST	5	INST	1½–2
FRUST	10	FRUST	2½+

Background Knowledge Assessment. Most everyone has played baseball or softball. Tell me what you know about this popular game. adequate ☐ inadequate ☐

A Great American Sport

The history of baseball shows that the game has changed a great deal since it was first played. In 1839, Abner Doubleday set up the rules for playing a baseball game.

Later on, uniforms appeared. The players wore long pants, a fancy white shirt, and a straw hat. The umpire wore a long coat, a tall silk hat, and carried a cane. Rakes, ax handles, and tree branches were used as bats.

The first World Series was played in 1903. Baseball fans wanted to see the top teams from the two major leagues play. The winners would be the champions of the baseball world.

Comprehension Check

(F) 1. ____ What year were the rules set up for baseball?
(1839)

(F) 2. ____ Several things were used as baseball bats, name two.
(Rakes or ax handles, tree branches)

(V) 3. ____ What does "fan" mean in this story?
(A person interested in a sport or movie star.)

(F) 4. ____ What were the first player uniforms like?
(Long pants, fancy shirts, straw hat)

(I) 5. ____ Why does professional baseball have a World Series?
(So two top teams can play or two teams play for the championship)

Scoring Guide Fourth

SIG WR Errors		COMP Errors	
IND	2	IND	0–1
INST	5	INST	1½–2
FRUST	10+	FRUST	2½+

Background Knowledge Assessment. Why is Driver Education an important class or program?

adequate ☐   inadequate ☐

Driver Education

Even our parents may have some bad driving habits. This is why young drivers should take lessons from trained teachers.

A recent story makes this point. A young driver had learned from an older one. While driving, a young driver felt his two right wheels go off the road. He yanked the car quickly back onto the road. As a result, the car turned over. A passenger in the car was killed. A trained teacher would have taught the driver not to slam on the brakes. And not to turn back onto the road too quickly.

One of the best ways to decrease traffic accidents is to have more driver education.

Comprehension Check

(F) 1. ____ What happened when the young driver yanked the car back onto the road?
(Car turned over)

(F) 2. ____ When the car turned over what happened to a passenger?
(Person was killed)

(F) 3. ____ What does "decrease" mean?
(Make smaller, less)

(I) 4. ____ Why is it better to take driving lessons from a trained teacher than an older driver?
(A trained teacher knows more about driver training)

(I) 5. ____ What caused the car to turn over?
(Two right wheels were caught or jammed on the pavement or road)

Scoring Guide   Fifth

SIG WR Errors		COMP Errors	
IND	2	IND	0–1
INST	6	INST	1½–2
FRUST	11	FRUST	2½ +

Background Knowledge Assessment.   If I use words such as white-tailed deer, meadows, woods and hunting what do you think about?   adequate ☐   inadequate ☐

Sentinels in the Forest

Many wild creatures that travel with their own kind know by instinct how to protect the group. One of them acts as a sentinel.

Hidden by the branches of a low-hanging tree, I once watched two white-tailed deer feeding in a meadow. At first, my interest was held by their beauty. But soon I noticed something which was quite unusual: they were taking turns at feeding.

One deer was calmly cropping grass, unafraid and at ease. The other, a sentinel, stood guard against enemies. The guard deer watched every movement and used its sensitive nostrils to "feel" the air. Not for a moment, during the half hour I spied upon them, did they stop their teamwork.

Comprehension Check

(F) 1. ____ Where was the author as he watched the deer?
(Hidden by branches of a low-hanging tree)

(V) 2. ____ What is a "sentinel"?
(One who stands guard)

(I) 3. ____ Why was the deer that was eating calm and unafraid?
(Knew the other deer or sentinel was standing guard)

(V) 4. ____ What do "used its sensitive nostrils to 'feel' the air" mean?
(Had a good sense of smell and was smelling the air for a scent of an enemy)

(V) 5. ____ What does "cropping grass" mean in the story?
(Eating the grass)

Scoring Guide Sixth

SIG WR Errors		COMP Errors	
IND	2	IND	0–1
INST	6	INST	1½–2
FRUST	11	FRUST	2½+

W.P.M.

/ 8940

Background Knowledge Assessment. What airport can you name? Tell me about this airport or any others.

adequate ☐   inadequate ☐

Modern Airports

In the earliest days of aviation, there was no need for airports. The light wood-and-cloth airplanes could take off and land in any level, open field.

In contrast to these simple airfields, the modern airport is almost a city in itself. There are many buildings and services for the convenience and comfort of the passengers.

Waiting rooms, restaurants, barbershops, post offices, banks, souvenir shops, florists, and even bowling alleys are likely to be located in the airport.

But the heart of the airport is still the area where the planes take off and land—the runways. Jet planes require very long runways—sometimes as much as two miles in length. Runways are paved with concrete to withstand the impact of planes weighing up to 375 tons hitting the ground at speeds between 110 and 140 miles per hour. Taxiways link the runways with each other and with terminal buildings.

Comprehension Check

(F) 1. ____ Why were airports unnecessary in the early days of aviation?
(Planes were light, slow, short take off, etc.)

(F) 2. ____ Name three customer services found at modern airports.
(Restaurants, barbershop, post office, bank, etc.)

(F) 3. ____ Approximately how heavy are the large jets?
(They weigh over 375 tons)

(I) 4. ____ Why do jets require long runways?
(Planes are heavy and fast, long stop and take off, etc.)

(V) 5. ____ What does "impact" mean?
(Violent contact, collision, etc.)

Scoring Guide   Seventh

SIG WR Errors		COMP Errors	
IND	3	IND	0–1
INST	7–8	INST	1½–2
FRUST	15	FRUST	2½+

W.P.M.

/ 9450

Background Knowledge Assessment. The author seems to have strong opinions about American sport cars. Before you read the story can you guess what they are?   adequate ☐   inadequate ☐

Sports Cars

To most laymen, a sports car is simply a vehicle with a flashy, streamlined body decorated with plenty of chrome. Such a vehicle, however, might easily be everything that an actual sports car should not be. It is the engineering features that the untrained eye does not observe which distinguish the true sports car from the bloated, over-chromed and highly colored dream cars that cruise along the American freeways on weekend afternoons.

The meticulously engineered features of a genuine sports car are those observed on the road rather than those idolized in the parking lots of country clubs. That which ordinarily is referred to as an American sports car would not be permitted to enter a European road race, because it would be too unsafe both for its own operator and for the other participants in a race. For another thing, it would be ridiculously outclassed for acceleration and road-ability under conditions of such competitive driving.

Comprehension Check

(V) 1. _____ What does the author mean by the word "laymen"?
(A person untrained in a specific field or area)

(F) 2. _____ What do most Americans think sports cars are?
(Flashy, decorated body, etc.)

(F) 3. _____ The American sports car, usually found on our highways, would not be permitted in European road races. Why not?
(Unsafe, not well engineered, etc.)

(V) 4. _____ What does "meticulously" mean?
(Extremely careful about details)

(I) 5. _____ What is the author's opinion of American sports cars?
(They are incorrect, misguided, etc.)

Scoring Guide   Eighth

SIG WR Errors		COMP Errors	
IND	3	IND	0–1
INST	7–8	INST	1½–2
FRUST	15	FRUST	2½+

Form D

Part 1 Graded Word Lists
Designed for High School Students and Adults

1

1 then

2 place

3 garbage

4 grow

5 birthday

6 don't

7 night

8 men

9 flowers

10 fire

11 her

12 eight

13 stopping

14 let's

15 frog

16 trucks

17 cannot

18 feet

19 garden

20 drop

2

1 mouth

2 boats

3 together

4 chipmunk

5 wheels

6 clang

7 slide

8 deer

9 both

10 room

11 horn

12 beautiful

13 sorry

14 climb

15 head

16 corn

17 strong

18 blows

19 that's

20 own

3

1 soup

2 remember

3 enemy

4 inventor

5 enough

6 unusual

7 disappointed

8 posture

9 hour

10 direction

11 escape

12 matter

13 unhappy

14 discover

15 turkeys

16 either

17 pencil

18 nail

19 senseless

20 clothes

4

1 barrel

2 nephew

3 experience

4 trousers

5 iron

6 ghost

7 groan

8 weight

9 pedal

10 machine

11 force

12 weather

13 island

14 predict

15 knowledge

16 spoon

17 dozen

18 exercise

19 bound

20 rooster

5

1 plateau

2 bore

3 vinegar

4 muscle

5 sandals

6 contest

7 freedom

8 examined

9 scarf

10 oars

11 octave

12 salmon

13 briskly

14 delicious

15 pacing

16 considerable

17 musical

18 scientist

19 amount

20 hymn

6

1 moisture

2 dorsal

3 envelope

4 request

5 knights

6 applause

7 culprit

8 demon

9 wreath

10 torrent

11 liberty

12 blond

13 marsh

14 customer

15 hearth

16 pounce

17 instinct

18 billows

19 sensitive

20 nostrils

7

1 plasma

2 alternative

3 barometer

4 joyous

5 dialects

6 mystical

7 taco

8 exploited

9 thermostat

10 vigorously

11 attainment

12 logical

13 geologist

14 resource

15 fundamental

16 compliment

17 carbonation

18 senators

19 condense

20 biscuits

8

1 coagulate

2 surgical

3 optimistic

4 disposition

5 metaphor

6 controversy

7 exchange

8 imperative

9 demeanor

10 futility

11 absolutely

12 foggy

13 ardently

14 perch

15 immortal

16 pliers

17 obsolete

18 speculate

19 admiral

20 keel

Form D

Part 2 Graded Paragraphs
Designed for High School Students and Adults

The Car Wash

Diane's car needed cleaning. She went to the car wash. The man asked what she wanted. "Just a wash," said Diane. The man asked, "How about gas?"

"No, just a wash," she said.

Then the man asked about hot wax. "No, just a wash," she said.

"Wow! People are always selling something," said Diane.

Lizards Are Smart

Lizards use many ways to protect themselves. Some lizards can blow up to three times their size. Others can keep running even if their tail is pulled off. All they do is just grow a new tail. There are even lizards that can swim.

Most lizards move in funny ways. They can walk or run upside-down. They can run on their two back legs. Lizards are quick and can leap from place to place.

If you don't think that lizards are smart, try to catch one.

Hang Gliding

Hang gliding? Some people think that this new sport is called hand gliding. "Hang," "hand"—it doesn't take much to cause confusion.

Hang gliding got its start in the early 1970s. California is likely to have the most hang glider pilots. Hang gliders are made by attaching a triangular sail to a frame. The glider is about 32 feet wide. The pilot takes off by holding the glider and running down the windward side of a cliff. When airborne, the pilot steers the glider with a control bar.

Hang glider pilots must be well trained. It is a good sport for both men and women.

Forest Fire Fighters

Fighting forest fires is hard work. Forest fires are difficult to stop when water is not available. Fire fighters have to use other ways to stop fires. They dig fire lines. This is a long cleared strip in front of the fire. The fire line keeps the flames from spreading. The fire line also holds the fire in a small area. Fire fighters work back from this line to put out the fire. Sometimes smoke jumpers are used to fight fires. They parachute into out-of-the-way places to put out fires. A new way to stop forest fires is called slurry bombing. Airplanes drop liquid in front of the fire to slow it down. With a lot of skill and a little luck, fire fighters can save our forests.

College Football

College football began when Princeton played Rutgers in 1869. Soon other colleges began playing football. Different rules were added each year. Some schools added passing. Others added scoring. Even the size of the field was different. Finally, in 1905 a national committee was formed. This committee made rules for all schools to follow.

In the early days football was a simple game. One team just ran the ball around or over the other. Today football is complex. It takes months for players to learn the plays. Colleges are grouped into conferences. For example, the winner of the PAC-10 and BIG 10 play each other in the Rose Bowl Game. Football is the most popular college sport. We all know when it's fall because football is everywhere.

Hey Kid, This Is the U.S. Open

It was 1979 when the big tennis event happened. Tracy Austin, age 16, won the U.S. Tennis Open. When Tracy beat Chris Evert, she became the youngest player to win the Open. No player, male or female, had ever won the Open at this young age.

Few people actually thought Tracy had a chance to win. Even her coach did not believe she could win. In fact, he vowed to quit smoking if she won. Tracy reminded him about the no smoking vow when the match was over.

Tracy Austin beat Evert by being steady and consistent. Evert was rocked by critical mistakes throughout the match. When the match was over Tracy shouted, "I can't believe it! I really did win!"

Burro Lift

What do you do with 400 burros who are over-grazing in Arizona's Grand Canyon? This was a difficult problem for the U.S. Park Service. As one person put it, "Those burros are in a hole a mile deep."

After thinking about many things, the U.S. Park Service decided to shoot the burros. A group called Fund for Animals opposed the Park Service plan. With the Park Service's OK, the group began removing the burros by helicopter. Rounding up burros in a hot canyon was a hard job. Another problem was flying them out of the canyon. Then came the greatest job of all, finding a new home for the burros.

The Fund for Animals group and another group, called the National Organization for Wild American Horses, put the burros up for adoption.

The most important thing about the burro lift was that when people decide to work together they can overcome problems.

The White Shark

Scientists tell us that there are about 350 kinds of sharks. Of this total, approximately ten percent are known to be man-eating. The most dangerous of the man-eating sharks is the white shark. This killer can grow up to 40 feet long and devour a six-foot man whole.

According to scientists, white sharks and other man-eaters rely on their nose to locate food. Scientists conducted two types of experiments to prove this. They starved a shark, then dropped a small amount of fish juice into the water. The shark immediately became excited. Scientists plugged up the nostrils of a man-eating shark. In this situation, the shark could not tell the difference between a bag of food and a bag of marbles.

No one knows why or when sharks will attack. The best advice for man is to leave sharks alone, especially white sharks.

Form D

Form D may be used in any of the following ways.

1. As a set of *silent paragraphs* for students who might reject oral reading

2. As a set of *silent paragraphs* used with Form C

3. As a set of *paragraphs* for assessing the student's listening capacity level. (see p. 8)

Form D Inventory Record

Summary Sheet

Student's Name _____ Grade _____ Age (Chronological) _____
yrs.　mos.

Date _____ School _____ Administered by _____

Part 1 Word Lists			Part 2 Graded Paragraphs			
Grade Level	Percent of Words Correct	Word Recognition Errors		SIG WR	Comp	L.C.
1	————	Consonants	PP			
		____ Consonants	P			
		____ blends	1			
		____ digraphs	2			
		____ endings	3			
		____ compounds	4			
		____ contractions	5			
2	————	Vowels	6			
		____ long	7			
		____ short	8			
		____ long/short oo				

____ vowel + r
____ diphthong
____ vowel comb.
____ a + 1 or w

Estimated Levels

Grade

Independent ____

Instructional ____ (range)

Frustration ____

Listening Capacity ____

3	————	Syllable
		____ visual patterns
		____ prefix
4	————	____ suffix
5	————	Word Recognition
6	————	reinforcement and
7	————	Vocabulary
8	————	development

Comp Errors

_____ Factual (F)

_____ Inference (I)

_____ Vocabulary (V)

_____ "Word Caller"
(A student who
reads without asso-
ciating meaning)

_____ Poor Memory

Summary of Specific Needs:

Permission is granted by the publisher to reproduce pp. 139 through 161.

1		2		3		4	
1 then	_____	1 mouth	_____	1 soup	_____	1 barrel	_____
2 place	_____	2 boats	_____	2 remember	_____	2 nephew	_____
3 garbage	_____	3 together	_____	3 enemy	_____	3 experience	_____
4 grow	_____	4 chipmunk	_____	4 inventor	_____	4 trousers	_____
5 birthday	_____	5 wheels	_____	5 enough	_____	5 iron	_____
6 don't	_____	6 clang	_____	6 unusual	_____	6 ghost	_____
7 night	_____	7 slide	_____	7 disappointed	_____	7 groan	_____
8 men	_____	8 deer	_____	8 posture	_____	8 weight	_____
9 flowers	_____	9 both	_____	9 hour	_____	9 pedal	_____
10 fire	_____	10 room	_____	10 direction	_____	10 machine	_____
11 her	_____	11 horn	_____	11 escape	_____	11 force	_____
12 eight	_____	12 beautiful	_____	12 matter	_____	12 weather	_____
13 stopping	_____	13 sorry	_____	13 unhappy	_____	13 island	_____
14 let's	_____	14 climb	_____	14 discover	_____	14 predict	_____
15 frog	_____	15 head	_____	15 turkeys	_____	15 knowledge	_____
16 trucks	_____	16 corn	_____	16 either	_____	16 spoon	_____
17 cannot	_____	17 strong	_____	17 pencil	_____	17 dozen	_____
18 feet	_____	18 blows	_____	18 nail	_____	18 exercise	_____
19 garden	_____	19 that's	_____	19 senseless	_____	19 bound	_____
20 drop	_____	20 own	_____	20 clothes	_____	20 rooster	_____
	_____ %		_____ %		_____ %		_____ %

Teacher note: If the student missed five words in any column—stop Part 1. Begin Graded Paragraphs, Part 2, (Form D), at highest level in which all 20 words were recognized. To save time, if the first ten words were correct, go on to the next list. If one of the first ten words were missed, continue the entire list.

Form D Part 1

5		6		7		8	
1 plateau	_____	1 moisture	_____	1 plasma	_____	1 coagulate	_____
2 bore	_____	2 dorsal	_____	2 alternative	_____	2 surgical	_____
3 vinegar	_____	3 envelope	_____	3 barometer	_____	3 optimistic	_____
4 muscle	_____	4 request	_____	4 joyous	_____	4 disposition	_____
5 sandals	_____	5 knights	_____	5 dialects	_____	5 metaphor	_____
6 contest	_____	6 applause	_____	6 mystical	_____	6 controversy	_____
7 freedom	_____	7 culprit	_____	7 taco	_____	7 exchange	_____
8 examined	_____	8 demon	_____	8 exploited	_____	8 imperative	_____
9 scarf	_____	9 wreath	_____	9 thermostat	_____	9 demeanor	_____
10 oars	_____	10 torrent	_____	10 vigorously	_____	10 futility	_____
11 octave	_____	11 liberty	_____	11 attainment	_____	11 absolutely	_____
12 salmon	_____	12 blond	_____	12 logical	_____	12 foggy	_____
13 briskly	_____	13 marsh	_____	13 geologist	_____	13 ardently	_____
14 delicious	_____	14 customer	_____	14 resource	_____	14 perch	_____
15 pacing	_____	15 hearth	_____	15 fundamental	_____	15 immortal	_____
16 considerable	_____	16 pounce	_____	16 compliment	_____	16 pliers	_____
17 musical	_____	17 instinct	_____	17 carbonation	_____	17 obsolete	_____
18 scientist	_____	18 billows	_____	18 senators	_____	18 speculate	_____
19 amount	_____	19 sensitive	_____	19 condense	_____	19 admiral	_____
20 hymn	_____	20 nostrils	_____	20 biscuits	_____	20 keel	_____
	_____ %		_____ %		_____ %		_____ %

W.P.M.

/3240

Background Knowledge Assessment. What things do you have to do when you wash a car?[19]

adequate ☐   inadequate ☐

The Car Wash

Diane's car needed cleaning. She went to the car wash. The man asked what she wanted. "Just a wash," said Diane. The man asked, "How about gas?"

"No, just a wash," she said.

Then the man asked about hot wax. "No, just a wash," she said.

"Wow! People are always selling something," said Diane.

Comprehension Check

(F) 1. ____ Who went to the car wash?
(Diane or a girl)

(I) 2. ____ About how old was this person (Diane)? If you are not sure, guess.
(At least sixteen or over sixteen years of age)

(F) 3. ____ What two things did the man want to sell?
(Gas and hot wax, car wash)

(V) 4. ____ What does "always selling something" mean?
(Trying to sell extra items, selling more)

(I) 5. ____ How did the person (Diane) feel about all the extra service offered?
(Surprised, didn't like it)

Scoring Guide   First

SIG WR Errors		COMP Errors	
IND	0	IND	0–1
INST	2	INST	1½–2
FRUST	4+	FRUST	2½+

19. See page 8 for a discussion of Background Knowledge Assessment.

Background Knowledge Assessment. Most zoos' have a variety of lizards. You probably know things about lizards. Tell me about them.

adequate ☐ inadequate ☐

Lizards Are Smart

Lizards use many ways to protect themselves. Some lizards can blow up to three times their size. Others can keep running even if their tail is pulled off. All they do is just grow a new tail. There are even lizards that can swim.

Most lizards move in funny ways. They can walk or run upside-down. They can run on their two back legs. Lizards are quick and can leap from place to place.

If you don't think that lizards are smart, try to catch one.

Comprehension Check

(F) 1. _____ Give two ways in which lizards protect themselves.
(Blow up or increase size, hide, move in funny ways, leap, etc.)

(V) 2. _____ Give a word that means about the same as "protect."
(Defend, guard, preserve)

(F) 3. _____ What happens to a lizard if its tail is pulled off?
(Nothing, grows another)

(F) 4. _____ Why is it hard to catch a lizard?
(They're smart, quick, and/or can leap)

(I) 5. _____ How does the author feel about lizards?
(Likes them, thinks they are smart)

Scoring Guide Second

SIG WR Errors		COMP Errors	
IND	1	IND	0–1
INST	4	INST	1½–2
FRUST	8+	FRUST	2½+

Background Knowledge Assessment. Hang (not hand) gliding is a new sport. Hang gliders use wind currents when gliding. What do you know about this new sport?   adequate ☐   inadequate ☐

Hang Gliding

Hang gliding? Some people think that this new sport is called hand gliding. "Hang," "hand" it doesn't take much to cause confusion.

Hang gliding got its start in the early 1970s. California is likely to have the most hang glider pilots. Hang gliders are made by attaching a triangular sail to a frame. The glider is about 32 feet wide. The pilot takes off by holding the glider and running down the windward side of a cliff. When airborne, the pilot steers the glider with a control bar.

Hang glider pilots must be well trained. It is a good sport for both men and women.

Comprehension Check

(F) 1. _____ What state is likely to have the most hang glider pilots?
(California)

(F) 2. _____ About how wide is a hang glider?
(Thirty-two feet)

(V) 3. _____ Describe a "triangular" sail.
(Three sides)

(F) 4. _____ How does a pilot change the direction of the glider?
(With a control bar)

(I) 5. _____ Why do hang glider pilots need to be well trained?
(Misjudge air, crash, person can get killed)

Scoring Guide Third

SIG WR Errors		COMP Errors	
IND	2	IND	0–1
INST	5–6	INST	1½–2
FRUST	11+	FRUST	2½+

Background Knowledge Assessment.   Forest fires are dangerous. Once a fire is started can you tell some ways to put the fire out?   adequate ☐   inadequate ☐

Forest Fire Fighters

Fighting forest fires is hard work. Forest fires are difficult to stop when water is not available. Fire fighters have to use other ways to stop fires. They dig fire lines. This is a long cleared strip in front of the fire. The fire line keeps the flames from spreading. The fire line also holds the fire in a small area. Fire fighters work back from this line to put out the fire. Sometimes smoke jumpers are used to fight fires. They parachute into out-of-the-way places to put out fires. A new way to stop forest fires is called slurry bombing. Airplanes drop liquid in front of the fire to slow it down. With a lot of skill and a little luck, fire fighters can save our forests.

Comprehension Check

(F) 1. _____ Why are forest fires difficult to stop?
(Lack of water to put out fires, fires in out-of-way places)

(F) 2. _____ What are fire lines?
(Long cleared strips which keep fires from spreading)

(I) 3. _____ If there were strong winds directly from the west, where would you put the fire line?
(On the east, facing the wind and fire)

(V) 4. _____ What is slurry?
(A liquid used to slow down or smother fires)

(F) 5. _____ What do smoke jumpers do?
(Jump-parachute to out-of-the-way fires, put out fires)

Scoring Guide   Fourth

SIG WR Errors		COMP Errors	
IND	2	IND	0–1
INST	6	INST	1½–2
FRUST	12+	FRUST	2½+

Background Knowledge Assessment. When I use words such as pass, tackle, run, cheerleaders, and quarterback you are probably thinking of football. Tell me about football.   adequate □   inadequate □

College Football

College football began when Princeton played Rut-gers in 1869. Soon other colleges began playing football. Different rules were added each year. Some schools added passing. Others added scoring. Even the size of the field was different. Finally, in 1905 a national committee was formed. This committee made rules for all schools to follow.

In the early days football was a simple game. One team just ran the ball around or over the other. Today football is complex. It takes months for players to learn the plays. Colleges are grouped into conferences. For example, the winner of the PAC-10 and BIG 10 play each other in the Rose Bowl Game. Football is the most popular college sport. We all know when it's fall because football is every-where.

Comprehension Check

(F) 1. ____ Can you name one of the first colleges to play football?
(Princeton or Rutgers)

(F) 2. ____ Why was a national athletic committee formed in 1905?
(To make rules or standardize the game of football)

(F) 3. ____ What was said that makes you think that football was simple in the early days?
(One team just ran around or over)

(I) 4. ____ How did they get the ball down the field before passing was allowed?
(Ran the ball)

(V) 5. ____ What is meant by "colleges are grouped into conferences"?
(A number of teams agree to work together or play each other)

Scoring Guide   Fifth

SIG WR Errors		COMP Errors	
IND	2	IND	0–1
INST	6	INST	1½–2
FRUST	12+	FRUST	2½+

Background Knowledge Assessment.   Tennis is another popular sport. Have you ever played tennis. Tell me about this sport.

adequate ☐   inadequate ☐

Hey Kid, This Is the U.S. Open

It was 1979 when the big tennis event happened. Tracy Austin, age 16, won the U.S. Tennis Open. When Tracy beat Chris Evert, she became the youngest player to win the Open. No player, male or female, had ever won the Open at this young age.

Few people actually thought Tracy had a chance to win. Even her coach did not believe she could win. In fact, he vowed to quit smoking if she won. Tracy reminded him about the "no smoking" vow when the match was over.

Tracy Austin beat Evert by being steady and consistent. Evert was rocked by critical mistakes throughout the match. When the match was over Tracy shouted, "I can't believe it! I really did win!"

Comprehension Check

(F) 1. _____ This story was about what young tennis player?
(Tracy Austin)

(F) 2. _____ How old was she when she won the U.S. Open?
(Sixteen)

(V) 3. _____ What does "vowed" mean?
(Agreed to do something, promised)

(I) 4. _____ Why did the coach probably have another feeling besides happiness after the win?
(He had to quit smoking)

(F) 5. _____ Why did Tracy beat Chris Evert?
(She was better, was consistent, didn't make as many mistakes)

Scoring Guide   Sixth

SIG WR Errors		COMP Errors	
IND	2	IND	0–1
INST	6	INST	1½–2
FRUST	12+	FRUST	2½+

Background Knowledge Assessment. Imagine getting burros out of Arizona's Grand Canyon. What problems would a group have if they tried to get burros out of the steep walled Grand Canyon?

adequate ☐   inadequate ☐

Burro Lift

What do you do with 400 burros who are over-grazing in Arizona's Grand Canyon? This was a difficult problem for the U.S. Park Service. As one person put it, "Those burros are in a hole a mile deep."

After thinking about many things, the U.S. Park Service decided to shoot the burros. A group called Fund for Animals opposed the Park Service plan. With the Park Service's OK, the group began removing the burros by helicopter. Rounding up burros in a hot canyon was a hard job. Another problem was flying them out of the canyon. Then came the greatest job of all, finding a new home for the burros.

The Fund for Animals group and another group, called the National Organization for Wild American Horses, put the burros up for adoption.

The most important thing about the burro lift was that when people decide to work together they can overcome problems.

Comprehension Check

(V) 1. ____ What is meant by over-grazing?
(Too much grass or vegetation is eaten, not enough food for other animals)

(I) 2. ____ Why not just walk the burros out of the Grand Canyon?
(Sides of Canyon too steep or it says a hole a mile deep)

(F) 3. ____ How did the U.S. Park Service plan to remove the burros?
(Shoot them)

(F) 4. ____ How did the Fund for Animals remove the burros?
(Flew them out by helicopter)

(V) 5. ____ Give me a word that means to work together or to work for a common purpose.
(Cooperate, association, etc.)

Scoring Guide   Seventh

SIG WR Errors		COMP Errors	
IND	3	IND	0–1
INST	7	INST	1½–2
FRUST	14+	FRUST	2½+

Background Knowledge Assessment. Did you see the movie Jaws? (If, yes, tell about it) (If no, have you seen a movie about sharks?)   adequate ☐   inadequate ☐

The White Shark

Scientists tell us that there are about 350 kinds of sharks. Of this total, approximately ten percent are known to be man-eating. The most dangerous of the man-eating sharks is the white shark. This killer can grow up to 40 feet long and devour a six-foot man whole.

According to scientists, white sharks and other man-eaters rely on their nose to locate food. Scientists conducted two types of experiments to prove this. They starved a shark, then dropped a small amount of fish juice into the water. The shark immediately became excited. Scientists plugged up the nostrils of a man-eating shark. In this situation, the shark could not tell the difference between a bag of food and a bag of marbles.

No one knows why or when sharks will attack. The best advice for man is to leave sharks alone, especially white sharks.

Comprehension Check

(F) 1. ___ About what percent of sharks are man-eating?
(10 percent)

(F) 2. ___ What do white sharks use to locate food?
(Their nose or smell)

(V) 3. ___ What does "experiment" mean?
(To prove, demonstrate, or find out something)

(F) 4. ___ In one experiment a man-eating shark could not tell the difference between food and marbles, why?
(Nostrils or nose plugged, couldn't smell anything)

(F) 5. ___ Why is it dangerous to bleed in water where sharks are?
(Can smell it)

Scoring Guide   Eighth

SIG WR Errors		COMP Errors	
IND	3	IND	0–1
INST	7	INST	1½–2
FRUST	14+	FRUST	2½+